Japan: The New Mix
Architecture, Interiors, and More

Original Japanese edition published in Japan in 2006
by Graphic-sha Publishing Co., Ltd.
1-14-17 Kudankita, Chiyoda-ku, Tokyo 102-0073 Japan
© 2006 Graphic-sha Publishing Co., Ltd.

English edition published in Australia in 2007 by
The Images Publishing Group Pty Ltd
ABN 89 059 734 431
6 Bastow Place, Mulgrave, Victoria, 3170, Australia
Phone +61 3 9561 5544 Fax +61 3 9561 4860
books@imagespublishing.com
www.imagespublishing.com

© 2007 The Images Publishing Group Ptd Ltd
The Images Publishing Group Reference Number: 726

National Library of Australia
Cataloguing-in-Publication entry
Takahashi, Masaaki.
Japan, the new mix.

ISBN 9781864702675

1. Architecture, Japanese - Pictorial works. I. Title.

720.952

Edited by Kumiko Sakamoto (Graphic-sha Publishing Co., Ltd.),
        Janelle McCulloch (Images Publishing)

Photographs of Architects and Interior Designers by Mikio Shuto
Art Direction and Design by Hideyuki Yamano
Design by Asumi Yoshino
English Text Layout by Shinichi Ishioka
English Translation by Alice Tallents

Printed by Everbest Printing Co., Ltd., China

Images has included on its website a page for special notices in relation
to this and our other publications.
Please visit: www.imagespublishing.com

Japan: The New Mix

Architecture, Interiors, and More

Masaaki Takahashi
Supervised by Klein Dytham architecture

Preface

Japanese architecture and design takes into account not only the degree of tolerance of the environment but also the weight of demands by the client to produce, in terms of both quality and quantity, a veritable kaleidoscope of sophisticated design on a level unparalleled in history.

Innovation in design and architecture is born from a flexible way of thinking that is no longer bound to history, and it was precisely the collapse of the bubble economy that created this fulcrum for new ideas. As renowned architects and designers flocked to Japan from overseas, the country became a testing ground for design, and the results of this experimentation is evident in the profusion of designs being churned out today.

For architects and interior designers born in the 1960s, the fact that they experienced the 1980s pre-bubble and bubble years has great significance, although the fact that the economic ebullience was over when designers born in the 1970s entered society and therefore missed out the bubble is also highly significant. For the former, seeing structures and interiors sprouting like mushrooms and living through the boom years as they happened provides them with a physical memory of the period that they exploit as a design resource. The latter on, the other hand, not only have access to the fruits of the bubble but, as inheritors of its aftermath, learned to operate in an environment that was not easy on architecture and interiors; facing circumstances that forced them to rack their brains for a new way of looking at things. As such, they tend to use this experience as a springboard for new ideas.

A look at the next generation of architects and interior reveals a group that, while operating in a field created by those born before the 1950s, consists primarily of designers born in the Sixties, joined by the younger generation from the Seventies. It is easy to imagine how they will forge ahead to produce a tide of new architectural design.

Masaaki Takahashi

Japan: The New Mix
Architecture, Interiors, and More

The Work of 21 Architects and
Interior Designers

01/

MOUNT FUJI ARCHITECTS STUDIO

Masahiro Harada + MAO

Abandoned for over 40 years, the rooftop of a beauty college in Tokyo's center of youth culture, Shibuya, was covered in wood decking and given a new lease of life as an open-air roof garden, complete with café. The designers behind this project, entitled Secondary Landscape, are architects Masahiro Harada and MAO, who together make up MOUNT FUJI ARCHITECTS STUDIO.

"In buildings and urban areas, each and every space is labeled and classified according to use, until the city is crammed full of minutely branded spaces. Thus the only place we found that was still uninscribed in downtown areas was the roof," explains Masahiro Harada, one half of the innovative duo.

MAO and Masahiro Harada's debut work, a DIY home called XXXX-House, was also visionary. Rather than being built in the traditional sense of the word, the structure is, as its name suggests, pieced together from a flexible system of modules made up of a number of identical units.

Light-Light Shelter, on the other hand, which is another of their projects, is a Japanese-style delicatessen elongated like a glass-ended tube to make the best use of available space. Sunlight enters through openings between trusses that provide the structure its rigidity, before being scattered by hyperbolic paraboloids in the shell roof to softly diffuse through the interior.

XXXX-House >>

XXXX-House

Ceramics studio / Yaizu City, Shizuoka Prefecture / 2003

Light-Light Shelter

Delicatessen / Yaizu City, Shizuoka Prefecture / 2004

Secondary Landscape

Roof garden and salon / Shibuya-ku, Tokyo / 2004

Story

MOUNT FUJI ARCHITECTS STUDIO's XXXX-House is a unique, DIY structure that costs the same as a new Toyota Corolla. Erected from a series of alternating rectangles and parallelograms, it looks a little like a concertina from the outside. There is something that sets this house apart from conventional buildings and, when you learn that Masahiro Harada's father used to design ships, you'd be forgiven for thinking it has a hint of the Ark about it.

Asked to share his thoughts on the subject, Harada comments, "A ship's environment, the ocean, is incredibly harsh. You can be faced with rough seas, storms and even struck by lightning. A ship has to stay afloat and protect the lives of its crew, so there's absolutely no scope for error. This means it's put together in an extremely logical way and, what's more, this dose of rationality keeps it from becoming too obtrusively comfort-oriented."

With his father designing vessels for a shipbuilding company located in Shimizu Port in central Japan's Shizuoka Prefecture, Masahiro Harada grew up surrounded by craftsmen and other professionals in the ship-building industry. His father's primary interest lay in identifying the optimum scale and materials for a space for people to live in, and then encasing it in an oversize, yet rationally constructed object like a ship.

"You know, I don't believe in the hypothetical 'space' talked about in architecture. In your head, you might imagine that a space—a cube for example—exists independently, but, if you think about it in everyday terms, it's really only brought into being by the objects surrounding it."

Instead of taking an abstract, enclosed space as his starting point, Harada looks at what is already there, conceiving a living area as the space that happens to exist between these pre-existing objects. "I guess you could say it's similar to the relationship between a ship and its internal environment," he says.

Harada's partner MAO was also heavily influenced by her father. When her father was young, he went to study in the States, where he ended up living next door to the then-unknown Yoko Ono. Upon returning home, he single-handedly undertook the interior design of an embassy before going on to work on parabolic antennas. As a child, she loved the time she spent with her dad leafing through flyers for new housing developments stuffed inside the local paper, imagining floor plans of their own. At high school, she discovered physics and quickly chose to specialize in science. "I was so good at it that I could just look at the answers and pick out the right one without doing all the calculations," she grins. When she was still a student, she became interested in the work of Atelier ZO and traveled as far as Hokkaido to work behind the desk for the design group.

In the meantime, her husband, having spent some time at Kengo Kuma and Associates, studied for 18 months in Barcelona on an artist's internship sponsored by the Japanese Agency for Cultural Affairs, before joining Arata Isozaki and Associates. The two finally met during MAO's senior year at college and in 2004 they established MOUNT FUJI ARCHITECTS STUDIO.

Their first project, XXXX-House, was designed for Masahiro Harada's father. Above all, they wanted to be involved in the physical process of the build themselves, and so the proposal was based on the idea of creating a system they could erect with their own hands. "We were intent on treating the structure like something off a production line. Architecture is an extension of carpentry, after all, and building a shelter is one of the most basic acts of any living creature. For this reason, it's something anyone can embark on. That's the message we're putting across."

While in most cases the concept for a piece of work is elaborated during initial planning stages, these two architects approach their work in terms of iconic forms and find the concept often declares itself as more of a postscript within the design flow. However, once a design has been completed, examination reveals it to have grown naturally from their particular themes and concerns. Focusing on craft-based conceptualization, Masahiro Harada and MAO's style consists of seeking out fresh approaches to conventional techniques.

02/

TORAFU ARCHITECTS

Koichi Suzuno + Shinya Kamuro

Rendering familiar objects into unfamiliar ones and presenting elements from the existing order in new combinations; you might say this is the golden rule of creative enterprise. The success of such an approach is certainly apparent in the innovative works dreamt up by the two young architects behind TORAFU: Koichi Suzuno and Shinya Kamuro.

One example of Torafu's work, simply entitled TEMPLATE IN CLASKA, can be found at the design-oriented Hotel Claska, in a long-stay guest room where the interior was inspired by draughtsman's templates. Here, the pair have invested humor into the space by slicing cutouts echoing the shapes of travelers' luggage and everyday essentials into the wooden surface of one wall. What results is an unexpectedly delightful storage style. In SPINNING OBJECTS, another of their designs, display units resembling immense potter's wheels seem to spin while floating in midair. And in UDS SHANGHAI OFFICE, the project em-ploys glass partitions with mirrored strips, enabling the designers to play on the subtle disappearance and reappearance of objects on the far side. Through this device, they were able to maximize the interplay of layers of images, as well as effects of light and shade. This visual ambiguity, where object and background become reversed in a kind of optical illusion realized in three-dimensions, is a quintessential example of TORAFU's pattern language.

The pair's persistent intellectual curiosity, tinged with a kind of innocence, has given rise to a succession of beguiling projects. SPINNING OBJECTS, for example, saw Suzuno bring to life an image he saw in *manga*, of which he is a huge fan. The architect also finds inspiration in his toy collection, accumulated gradually over the years, while partner Kamuro is a modern art buff. Their ideas, welling up from very different sources from those used by architects of the past, have resulted in some fascinating work.

TEMPLATE IN CLASKA

TEMPLATE IN CLASKA

Hotel guest room / Meguro-ku, Tokyo / 2004

SPINNING OBJECTS

Showroom / Chofu City, Tokyo / 2004

TABLE ON THE ROOF

Hotel rooftop multi-purpose space / Meguro-ku, Tokyo / 2004

ReBITA

Office / Shibuya-ku, Tokyo / 2005

UDS SHANGHAI OFFICE

Office / Shanghai, China / 2005

Story

The office of Koichi Suzuno + Shinya Kamuro, TORAFU, takes up one room on the top floor of Hotel Claska in Meguro, Tokyo, which is also the home of the duo's debut work, TEMPLATE IN CLASKA. For them, it is the perfect environment in which to work.

"Designers of our generation operate in a totally new environment, making use of the Internet to put their work and ways of thinking out there, which means that everyone inspires each other. Not many people know how much information on fascinating structures you can gain access to online. This kind of thing just wasn't available to earlier generations of designers," explains Suzuno.

Indeed, the current young generation of architects benefits from strong horizontal ties within the industry, disseminating information through blogs and other media, adding links to their friends' sites, and socializing together. When TEMPLATE IN CLASKA was first written up in *Frame*, the Dutch trade magazine for interior architecture and design, the international response was overwhelming and TORAFU received mail from young international architects intent on getting a job at a company producing such innovative design. In the past, Suzuno has also traveled as far as Melbourne to meet with an Australian architect, an ex-colleague who greatly inspired him when they worked together. For a period, he joined Kerstin Thompson Architects, to build up his professional experience. During that time, he also saw his bid for the Australian Garden Visitors' Center win the design competition and become a reality.

"I was only there in Australia for a year and a half, but managed to cram the experiences of ten years into my stay. When I was working in Japan, it was normal for me to catch the last train home every night, or even spend the night in the office. In Australia, however, by focusing on work during office hours and keeping my time at home for relaxation, I was able to further refine my practice. What's more, having this distance from Japan allowed me to look at it more objectively."

TORAFU came into being shortly after Suzuno arrived back from Australia, when a college friend, chosen to oversee the production of Hotel Claska, invited him to carry out the remodeling of suites for long-term guests in a project that would subsequently become known as TEMPLATE IN CLASKA. During his search for a partner, Suzuno called on an acquaintance, Kamuro, who had set up independently after working for several firms, culminating with Jun Aoki & Associates. Under Aoki, Kamuro spent two years supervising designs for Louis Vuitton before reaching the four-year maximum contract period allowed under the design firm's employment system.

In the world of architecture, where such an apprenticeship system is common, it is unusual to see someone go it alone at such a young age. As far as division of labor goes, in general, Suzuno directs the project as a whole, while Kamuro deals with the structural side of things, putting the finishing touches to each design. The story behind their company name is also unique. Since TEMPLATE IN CLASKA features a kennel complete with robot-dog AIBO, they needed to come up with a name to go on Sony's webpage featuring the hotel room. Wanting, in their idiosyncratic way, to go for a name with no apparent meaning, the pair plumped for TORAFU, a word they made up on the spur of the moment.

A fan of modern art, especially installation pieces, Kamuro tries to get around as many exhibitions as he can. A recent favorite is Olafur Eliasson. "In his work entitled "Beauty," lights are trained on a fine mist falling in a darkened room; it's an incredibly simple concept, but one that results in an uncanny piece of work that reveals rainbow bands of color depending on where you stand," he says. "In art today, rather than attempting to create something entirely new, there's a trend to instead present existing objects in a new light."

Both architects also love *manga*. A clue to the horizontal slicing of the display units in showroom design SPINNING OBJECTS apparently lies in the segmented and severed bodies found in graphic artist Hitoshi Iwaaki's series Parasyte, which goes to show just how far young designers today reject intellectual snobbery.

"Rather than an ideology, what's important to us is searching out something interesting and then making it a reality, irrespective of genre," reveals Suzuno. "This is because the most enjoyable aspect of working as an architect, and the thing we get a real sense of satisfaction from, is to see the things we've designed take on physical form."

The pair's most recent undertaking is the design for an 18,000-square-meter super resort on China's southernmost resort island, Hainan. Just how far their sense of humor will take them on such a large-scale work is a subject for curiosity.

03/

NAP Architects

Hiroshi Nakamura

Whatever the project, Hiroshi Nakamura aims to create "architecture scaled to life," emphasizing sensory perception and the experience of being in that precise location. Believing that the masculine principles colonizing the world of traditional architecture have reached their limits, Nakamura distances himself from the practice of erecting structures slavishly rooted in logic, preferring instead to adopt a strategy of prioritizing physical experience and ecopsychology. While young architects have pursued different methodologies and styles, Nakamura's decision to ground his conceptualizations in physical sensation makes it appear that he is working to revive an architecture that can be shared by many.

Rather than resulting from a superficial pursuit of form for form's sake, both the wall of a private house, swollen like a kangaroo's pouch, and a beauty salon's floor plan, whose lines strongly echo an ant's nest, were, in fact, the inevitable outcome of applying a certain rational concept to the builds. One of the leading figures of the post-bubble generation, Nakamura seems to be striking out across the ocean of consumerism, attempting to create a new image of the architect.

LANVIN BOUTIQUE GINZA

Boutique / Chuo-ku, Tokyo / 2004

House SH

Private residence / Minato-ku, Tokyo / 2005

Lotus Beauty Salon

Beauty salon / Kuwana City, Mie Prefecture / 2006

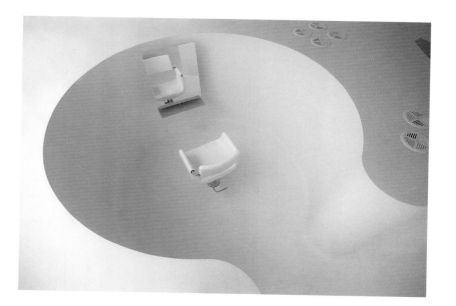

Story

On the main Chuo Dori avenue of Tokyo's affluent Ginza quarter stands Maison LANVIN, Hiroshi Nakamura's 2004 architectural debut. From outside, it looks as though a small black cabin has been introduced into the ground floor of an ordinary, glass-fronted building. Exterior walls of corduroy steel have been punched with roughly 3000 holes measuring 5 to 7.5 centimeters in diameter, which are then plugged with transparent acrylic. Designer Nakamura visualizes these apertures as tiny "peepholes" or perhaps private show windows; and explains that his aim was to bring the focus to bear solely on the beauty of the light shining through them.

Light entering via these windows fills the interior with dots of light that sparkle like diamonds. The quality of light changes with the weather and time of day and, at night, light glimmers through the openings onto the street to create a stunning exterior. In-house designers usually undertake the interior design for brand boutiques but in this case Nakamura was placed in charge of everything. Before involving him in the project for the Ginza branch, LANVIN's designer, Albert Elbaz, summoned Nakamura to Paris, taking him around his favorite interiors, including the opera house, fragrance shops, and cafés, and talking to him about the appeal of emotional spaces. This experience triggered a stronger expression of the artistic inclinations and sensitivities already at work in Nakamura's thinking.

During his childhood, Nakamura became obsessed with a book of architectural blueprints his parents had. From elementary school onwards, he aspired to become an architect and never diverged from this goal. At college, his interests lay not in speculative architectural theory, but in what you could physically achieve with architecture. A competition fanatic, Nakamura won over two million yen from design competitions while he was still a student. At a prizewinners' party, he became acquainted with Kengo Kuma and was invited to join his company. Far from merely being open to debating the function of the architect and role of architecture in society, Nakamura actually attempts to address these concepts within his own practice.

"While many architects have an image of the master architect as a god-like figure dictating plans from above, I believe there is an increasing need for architecture that emphasizes the psychological and corporeal experience of the person on the ground," he elucidates. "I feel that if you allow architecture to act as a tool allowing people to come into contact with structures in an affectionate way, the built environment will neither been seen as overpowering, nor simply as a flow, and instead a more intimate relationship can develop."

House SH was conceived as a new member of the family, or a "beloved character." The smooth bump in the main wall is unique; it becomes a space inviting "communication between the body and the wall"-a recess where family members can sit or recline. Standing on a plot measuring a scant five meters across, it was impossible to make this two-bedroom house particularly large, yet the molded wall acts to obscure the real dimensions of the structure, making it feel more spacious.

For the Lotus Beauty Salon, another of his projects, marketing concepts inspired Nakamura to propose a structure cocooning customers in what feels like their own private space, by fitting just 16 booths into a site measuring 330 square meters. Since completely isolating each treatment area would have had a negative impact on service and communication between staff, prevent ease of movement through the space as a whole and make each booth feel claustrophobic, the architect instead opted for curved partition walls. The floor descends gradually from the entrance towards the far end of the salon and the height of the partitions varies accordingly, ranging from half a meter at their lowest point to 1.4 meters at their highest. This makes them the perfect height to form bench seating in the entrance waiting area while, elsewhere, they rise above the head of seated clients, yet still allow standing staff to cast an eye over the entire salon.

Each booth is circular in shape, its size calculated as a function of the movement of the beautician around the centrally placed chair. The corners of interior walls have been softened into curves and painted in a variety of delicately graduated hues that melt away boundaries between floor and walls, making the space feel more airy. Here, Nakamura has subverted our habit of using changes in tangent and texture between surfaces to ascertain depth. Knowing that features of a person's immediate environment suggest how it should be interacted with, Nakamura has borrowed psychological analyses of affordance to create a design where the body and space are in a state of continual dialogue.

Maquette for a commercial complex
Kuwait, completion expected 2009

House SH

04/

TONERICO: INC.

Hiroshi Yoneya +
Ken Kimizuka +
Yumi Masuko

The greatest strength of TONERICO, which was launched by Hiroshi Yoneya, Ken Kimizuka, and Yumi Masuko in 2002, is that it offers expertise not only in architecture but also interior design and coordination. This enables this company to provide a kaleidoscope of design solutions encompassing every stage of the process, from erecting the skeleton of the building to coordinating interior fixtures and accessories.

Each new work by the design outfit reveals a new facet of their style: a juice bar where the mirror-finished steel façade reflects the bustling crowd of Shinjuku station; a Japanese confectionery store whose lighter-than-air display is hard to forget; a shop where color is combined to great effect with a grid pattern; a tranquil condo full of exquisite hues, and a deceptively simple installation in which numbers radiate light.

The Japanese confectionary store KIKYOYA is a prime example of what

the group can achieve when entrusted with every aspect of the job, from construction through to the smallest details of the interior. Water, a vital ingredient in *wagashi* Japanese-style confectionary, is coupled with polished stainless steel in a central design feature that's revealed as you step through the *noren* curtains at the entrance. Welling forth from the top, the water brims over to flow downwards across the faintly distorted surfaces; at times branching off into separate rivulets; at times running together as it traces its rippling path down the gleaming sides of the box. The sculpture is a subtle expression of *wagashi*, whose flavors are so delicate that even changes in the weather can affect the way they taste. Its mirror-like surfaces reflect the light, making a strong impression on the viewer that rises above any purely commercial intentions. Herein lies the essence of TONERICO's design.

ANYA

Wagashi store and teahouse / Setagaya-ku, Tokyo / 2004

JUS de COEUR

Juice bar / Shinjuku-ku, Tokyo / 2005

KIKYOYA

Wagashi store and teahouse / Nagoya City, Aichi Prefecture / 2005

MEMENTO @ le bain

Installation / Minato-ku, Toyko / 2005

TAMATOSHI + ACRYS

Showroom / Chiyoda-ku, Tokyo / 2005

Story

Shu Ha Ri: Mastering the art

One of TONERICO's outstanding works from the early days is ANYA, a Japanese *wagashi* store located in Seijo, Tokyo. Traditional Japanese-style design lends the space a serene atmosphere, creating an interior that won a number of interior design industry awards.

"We poured everything we had learnt from our experiences up to that point into the piece, to create something that would express an ideal of traditional design. We weren't intentionally seeking to create something strongly individualistic as such," says Yoneya, one third of TONERICO.

He explains their trajectory in terms of the phrase *Shu Ha Ri*, which was first penned by tea master Sen Rikyu in a poem illustrating the natural progression from acolyte to master. This journey, relevant to any discipline, encompasses three stages: Shu, learning the fundamentals from the master; Ha, breaking with tradition; and Ri, transcending the student-master relationship to become a master in your own right.

"First, you must stick to the rules and practices you have learnt. The result was ANYA in our first year of business. In the second year, you have to destroy what you have learnt so far, or you will never move on. The best example of this is GUSHA, our chair constructed of folded sheet steel, which represented a shift away from conventional practice. In the third year, you distance yourself from what you've built up so far. We wanted to see just how high we could soar when we left behind tradition."

Born of this process was MEMENTO, which distilled the essence of space design into an installation that went beyond language, defying definition as furniture or product. When exhibited at the 2005 Milano Salone Satellite, MEMENTO astounded visitors with its creative ingenuity. It was awarded the top prize of the Salone Satellite and TONERICO was catapulted into the limelight.

TONERICO's three designers first met when they became connected to Shigeru Uchida's design office, Studio 80. As a high school student, Hiroshi Yoneya had been interested in fashion, but was drawn more to shop interiors than the clothes themselves. It was later, during his time at the Department of Industrial, Interior and Craft Design at Musashino Art University, that something by Shigeru Uchida caught his eye at a furniture exhibition. "Those were the bubble years, when loud, toy-like furniture with a postmodern decorative feel was the rage. But Uchida's work was so direct, coming at you with pure elements: yellow, steel, folds, circles and squares! I really liked how simple and sturdy it was," he recalls. Having gained an introduction via a student above him, Yoneya started working part-time at Studio 80, later becoming a permanent member of staff. Meanwhile, Ken Kimizuka had graduated from Musashino Art University's Department of Architecture in the College of Art and Design. In his sophomore year, he too managed to get a part-time job at Studio 80. While majoring in ceramics at Joshibi University of Art and Design, Yumi Masuko worked part-time in an up-and-coming noodle bar called Sorori in Tokyo's affluent Nishi-Azabu district. The man responsible for Sorori's interior design was none other than Shigeru Uchida, with Setsuko Yamada in charge of coordination. Thanks to an introduction by the owner of the noodle bar, Masuko landed herself an apprenticeship under Yamada and was to remain the coordinator's assistant for the next 10 years. As well as her role as director of Tokyo Lifestyles Institute Inc., Yamada is now also the co-ordinator for luxury Ginza department store Matsuya and acts as a judge for Japan's long-standing Good Design Award as well. She has been friends with Uchida since they were students, and this connection was to provide Masuko's link to Studio 80. One year, after Uchida had become involved in creating so-called designer's mansions (stylish apartments designed by renowned architects), he was unhappy with the work done by the coordinator of a certain developer, and invited Masuko to take over. Soon after, Masuko met Yoneya at Studio 80, an encounter that later led to their marriage. Yoneya worked for Studio 80 for 10 years in all, rising to a position as chief designer. He happened to meet newly recruited Kimizuka just when he was considering setting up independently.

According to Yoneya, "When you are designing something, you always have a message that you want to get across to the viewer. What we felt strongly with MEMENTO was that if you have a clear purpose in mind, you might not necessarily end up with a good design, but even without clear practical use for the piece, you could still come up with something incredibly powerful. This is also a really important aspect of design." Rather than simply being satisfied with the functionality of so-called fine design, the three aim to stir up emotion in the viewer, communicating a message that transcends the physical existence of the object concerned.

05/

SKSK architects

Keiichiro Sako

Born in 1970, Keiichiro Sako established his Beijing office at the age of 34, and now employs a large number of Chinese and Japanese staff. He produces designs for a wide variety of projects, from condominiums, commercial complexes, and other large-scale urban developments to small stores and interiors. In one of his designs, a rainbow-colored band weaves its way through the interior of a Beijing children's bookstore. The story goes that Sako's eyes were first opened to the possibilities of color during his time as a visiting scholar at Columbia University, while this particular work also has its roots in childhood memories of vivid rainbows.

The bustling streets of China's cities provide another source of inspiration. Touched by what he sees there, Sako strives to foster architecture and urban development on a human scale. Working abroad also allows Sako to maintain a distance from Japanese design, with its oversensitivity to prevailing fashions, and create designs free from the constraints and stereotypes that might otherwise hamper his work.

T in Tokyo

Handcrafted jewelry shop / Shibuya-ku, Tokyo / 2003

FELISSIMO in Beijing

Boutique / Beijing, China / 2004

Kid's Republic in Beijing

Bookstore / Beijing, China / 2005

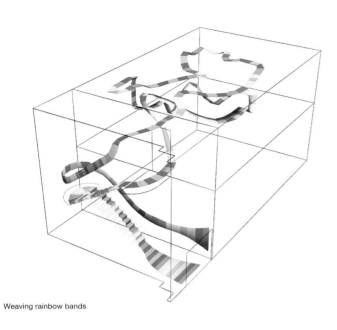

Weaving rainbow bands

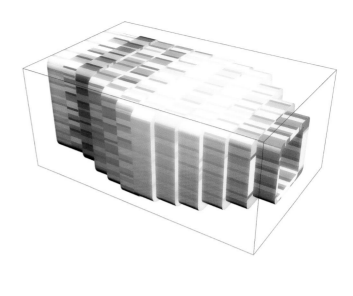

Wrapped rainbow bands

Storage in Tokyo

Storage space and offices / Koto -ku, Tokyo / 2005

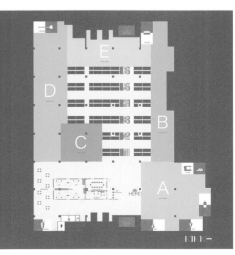

Top: Bumps in Beijing (housing complex and department store)
Beijing, China, completion expected 2007

Bottom: Lattice in Beijing (commercial complex)
Beijing, China, completion expected 2007

Story

After graduating from Tokyo Institute of Technology's graduate school, Keiichiro Sako entered employment in the offices of Riken Yamamoto and Field Shop. At the time, the company was bidding for contract after contract to build large-scale public facilities, and recruiting heavily. One 2003 project overseen by Sako was Shinonome Canal Court. This large-scale development was undertaken at a time when Japan's Urban Development Corporation was making way for the Urban Renaissance Agency, and the image they came up with reflected this shift away from conventional public housing towards condominium-style complexes. The master architect was Riken Yamamoto himself, who, alongside Sako, poured huge amounts of energy during the planning stages into designing the pared-down "basic units" outlined in the concept. Today, one of these units, with its glass entrance hall and window-side kitchen and bathroom, is Sako's second home.

In 2000, a call came from Yamamoto, in Beijing on a lecture tour. Explaining that there had been a call for tender and that he wanted put forward a design proposal, he asked Sako to join him in China as soon as possible. The project was on a massive scale, measuring 700,000 square meters in total and, at $150,000, the cost of submitting a design for the competition was correspondingly high. Intrigued by Yamamoto's lecture, a young developer had spoken to him about the large-scale development project planned for the capital's downtown area. Participation was by nomination only, but Riken Yamamoto outshone the competition to win the bid and Sako stepped on his first flight to China in September 2000.

The Beijing project consisted of the design and supervision of Jianwai Soho, a site named after the main

Jianguomenwai Dajie Avenue nearby. Situated in the capital's central business district, the site measured 120,000 square meters and the finished complex was to boast 700,000 square meters of floor space, housing retail, residential, and office premises. The build comprised seven stages in total and Sako acted as project leader under Yamamoto for stages one to three of construction, providing direct onsite supervision of 200,000 square meters. It wasn't until 2004 that he witnessed completion of the third stage. While all this was going on, Sako had also taken on the design for a tiny jewelry workshop in Hiroo through a friend. This project lay at the other end of the spectrum, with the premises measuring a mere 20 square meters, or one ten-thousandth of the area of the Jianwai Soho site.

As a result, Sako found himself carrying out intense discussions onsite in Beijing at the same time as pushing ahead with the Tokyo job through a process of long-distance trial and error. "At the time, I had no experience of working on interiors, particularly those for commercial premises, so didn't know exactly how to feel my way into the job, but when I focused in on the materials, it got a lot more interesting, and I eventually hit on using mirror-finished stainless steel for the façade."

By sending his instructions from Beijing to the building contractors in Tokyo, Sako was able to bring the tiny project to fruition through what was, in effect, a process of remote handling. T in Tokyo's façade reflects nearby stop-lights in a curious, random fashion, while tables inside feature a two-dimensional pattern that appears to float in 3D above their surfaces. Stainless steel extends from the façade along one wall of the interior, its looping, ground-in pattern producing an intricate effect impossible to capture on film.

As the Jianwai Soho project gradually came to an end, the designer arranged to spend a year as a visiting scholar at

Columbia University. At the end of 2003, however, Sako was contacted by two Chinese entrepreneurs and invited to work independently on a couple of projects. No sooner had he set up his own design office than he took on two sizeable jobs: the Kaleidoscape commercial facilities in Tianjin, and the building to house Jinhua city's Transport Bureau. At the same time as getting these projects off the ground, Sako moved to the States to start his research at Columbia University, and so commenced a particularly hectic period in his career.

"The work I'm doing now, creating architecture for urban spaces, is something I've been fascinated with since I was a student," he explains. "Riken Yamamoto, in his design for Ryokuentoshi, looked at how architecture engages with the city. His concept was to create a mechanism linking individual structures that would generate the city as it expanded. Right now, I am also lucky enough to be able to realize projects on a municipal scale, and to have reached the point where this is my job and I can tackle it in my own way."

KALEIDOSCAPE in Tianjin
(Commercial complex / Tianjin, China / 2005)

06/

Tezuka Architects

Takaharu + Yui Tezuka

"We want to demonstrate exactly what architecture is capable of," declare Takaharu and Yui Tezuka. "Take Le Corbusier, for example. His pilotis transcend the city's chaotic skyline and were surrounded by greenery, but they've ended up as parking towers in Japan."

Takaharu and Yui Tezuka see this as a failure of the modernist goal. Their solution? Going back to the roots of modern design and conceiving of an ideal architecture.

Within the requirements they are given, the Tezukas design houses that maximize contact with the open air, allowing you to feel close to nature. In their designs they have focused on a variety of other goals, such as putting the surrounding views to good use, letting in fresh breezes, getting rid of struts and partitions, making the roof into a viable living space, and creating aesthetic integrity with adjacent structures. Their work can be summed up in one word: comfort. Yet this comfort is never static; rather, it takes on different incarnations according to the distinctive personality of each residence.

The Tezukas have some key points in common: both their fathers worked in architecture, and they were brought up in houses that their fathers had designed. Furthermore, their childhood homes happen to be remarkably similar, each boasting plenty of windows and surrounded by greenery.

<< Echigo-Matsunoyama
Museum of Natural Science
Matsunoyama, Niigata

Echigo-Matsunoyama Museum of Natural Science Matsunoyama, Niigata

Natural science museum / Tokamachi City,
Niigata Prefecture / 2003

Roof House

Private residence / Kanagawa Prefecture / 2001

Engawa House

Private residence / Tokyo / 2003

Observatory House

Private residence / Kanagawa Prefecture / 2004

Eaves House

Private residence / Saitama Prefecture / 2006

Story

While he was working at Richard Rogers Partnership in London, Takaharu Tezuka visited the house in Wimbledon that Rogers designed for his parents. Along with his wife and other colleagues, Tezuka was there to celebrate Roger's mother's birthday. This house, constructed in 1967, represented the New English House at the Paris Biennale of the same year. Practically a cube, it stands on a long, thin plot in a leafy area of the city. The structure is steel framed, its interior painted a dramatic canary yellow with the doors finished in green. Both front and back walls are made entirely of glass, while the sides are constructed of sandwich panels made from an aluminum skin over a plastic core. Inside, the layout is simple, consisting of a kitchen island and sliding partition walls. The feeling of openness and affinity with the environment created by Rogers has many similarities with the techniques used by the Tezukas in their own designs. Their recent Engawa House, for example, could be seen as a bold extension of such an approach.

"We were really influenced by Rogers' parents' house. It was the first time I'd seen a house and understood what a housing concept really was," he admits. "You know, Rogers is often cited as a high-tech architect, but the Rogers we knew was a modernist." And it is true that the name Richard Rogers conjures up images of the Lloyds building, Pompidou Center, or other mechanical, factory-like structures, rather than his earlier works.

One thing that the couple learned from their four-year stint in the UK was the importance of quality of life. Richard Rogers' office was located in a 150-year-old building on the banks of the River Thames, and the sunsets over the water were a sight to behold. On weekends, they went to jazz clubs, enjoyed the view overlooking the river from the top of hills in Richmond Park, and went for walks around the city; having a wonderful time without feeling the need to spend much money.

"In the UK, things steadily accumulate from previous generations and become stored up in society. There's no need to keep re-building houses so there are fewer new developments; instead, people change the interiors but the structures live on. This means that there's more of an emphasis on quality. Japan, on the other hand, is a real throwaway society."

The Tezukas say that it was through this kind of hands-on experience that they gained the kind of deep understanding of the essentials of architecture that graduate studies or book learning just couldn't provide. "What we learned was not about architecture as such, but what architecture can engender." In their former lifestyle in Japan, they ought to have been taking time out to relax too, but of course hadn't realized this until they looked back.

The Tezukas returned to Japan in 1994. On the way home from Narita airport, they looked out of the window at the scenery passing by, and felt extremely disillusioned. "It was only after World War II that homes in Japan came to be rebuilt every 30 years or so; before that houses were lived in for many more years. As architects, we want to leave behind timeless buildings that'll live on into the future."

Takaharu Tezuka stresses that the key lies not in the shape or design of the actual structure, but in what happens to the things that enter it, and what it will be used for. "Architects can use their initiative to create lifestyle possibilities that didn't exist before. That's what's interesting. If you take Roof House, for example, it wasn't just about the house for the client but the lifestyle. Getting this idea about creating a lifestyle over to the general public and making it intelligible is really important."

"What's fascinating is to recapture a memory of a forgotten house, or create a building that makes an entirely new lifestyle possible. Architecture itself becomes the mechanism by which to achieve this. That's what we wanted to take a shot at doing."

One of the things the couple looks forward to is being invited over for dinner by the owners of the houses they design. With evident pleasure, they recount how one of their houses made such an impression on a child who grew up in it that the person went on to study architecture at university.

Fuji Kindergarten
Tachikawa City, Tokyo, completion expected 2007

07/

GLAMOROUS Co., Ltd.

Yasumichi Morita

The men's jewelry store SJX in Tadao Ando-designed Omotesando Hills; ZETTON CAFE & EATS in Aichi prefecture's Central Japan International Airport; the remodeled chateau restaurant Jöel Robuchon in Ebisu Garden Place; store and environment design for the interior of Tokyo Building TOKIA in the Marunouchi business district; Aoyama's DEAN & DELUCA store; a black diamond watch for Seiko... the list of Yasumichi Morita's talked-about designs never ends. His restaurants, boutiques, and cafés are always at the cutting edge of their time, and plotting them on a map lets you tell at a glance where Japan's design hot spots are, as well as where the money is.

While the growing interest in interiors and awareness of the names of individual designers among the general public may be a recent phenomenon, inside and outside the industry, Morita's name has never been far from the top of the list. But Morita's success is not solely attributable to the massive gourmet and restaurant boom that hit Japan around the time he made his design debut. Even now, there is no stopping the tidal wave of job offers he receives. The reason lies in the fact that he interprets everyday objects using his own particular brand of glamour, and is constantly aware of how to make creating something the user will find pleasure in.

MEGU New York

Japanese restaurant / New York, USA / 2004

ZETTON CAFE & EATS

Café / Central Japan International Airport, Aichi Prefecture / 2005

TOKIA (Tokyo Building)

Public space design for a commercial complex's basement,
second, and third floors / Chiyoda-ku, Tokyo / 2005

SJX

Men's jewelry and accessory shop / Shibuya-ku, Tokyo / 2006

MEGU Midtown

Japanese restaurant / New York, USA / 2006

Story

Yasumichi Morita arrives early for our interview and can be found seated at the counter of Omotesando's Carmenere, a wine bar whose interior he created. The designer is wearing a tight-fitting, glossy black jacket over a T-shirt paired with slim black pants; his trademark long hair and oversized glasses just another feature of his inimitable style. Morita lights a cigarette plucked from a gold cigarette case engraved with a lion's head. A connoisseur of champagne and tobacco, he has also designed a smoking room from the point of view of the heavy smoker.

"Somehow, I've always been surrounded by stylish people. Halfway through the 1980s, around the time everyone was still crazy for certain DC brands and there wasn't an Armani or Versace store in sight, my friends were making trips to Europe to bring back those kinds of labels. They looked so cool that I began to want some too and realized there was nothing for it but to get a job."

It wasn't that Morita started out with any particular interest in design or window displays; instead, the thing that set him on the path to becoming an interior designer was the simple desire to save up money for western labels. "I was doing all kinds of part-time jobs, and then someone suggested window dressing had a better hourly rate because it had to be done at night," says Morita, readily admitting that his ulterior motive for taking the job was getting together some cash. Even before he was first turned on to Versace at the age of 16, he was a delinquent, but a stylish delinquent.

Morita undertook his first interior design project when he was an 18-year old college student holding down several part-time window-dressing jobs. It was a solid first piece that can be tracked down in Kobe's Sannomiya district, in a bar called COOL that still boasts the original interior. "At the time, Sannomiya was divided between the poles of grungy American and ultra-conservative styles; there was no middle ground," he explains. The image Morita had in mind was a basement bar that wouldn't look out of place on the streets of New York, a place to have a beer at a reasonable price with soul playing in the background. One night, he found a kindred spirit in the owner of a bar and Morita round himself being given free reign to produce the interior as he saw fit. Not long after, he met the CEO of design office Imagine, who was won over by his confidence, and found himself working full-time.

"I guess it was because I was surrounded by a crowd of interesting people all living it up that a lot of opportunities came my way," he explains. Since he'd never gone to design school, however, he had to teach himself basics like technical drawing. He learned a lot of what he knows from people working in the industry.

"There aren't so many scary carpenters around anymore, but when I was starting out they used to teach by tearing my designs to pieces. When I look back, I see that I was turning up them with cartoon-style drawings. They'd take one look, then growl, 'So you think you can make this?!' and throw it straight back at me. Even so, they taught me a hell of a lot, you know? They'd give me tips, then tell me to bring it back in another 10 minutes."

Morita established his eponymous

NETSURETSU, HEP NAVIO

Chinese restaurant / Kita-ku, Osaka / 1996

Ken's Dining, Shinjyuku

Fusion restaurant / Shinjuku-ku, Tokyo / 1999

Kansai-based design office in 1996, but it wasn't until he designed the interior for Kenichiro Okada's Chinese restaurant, Netsuretsu Shokudo in Umeda, Osaka, that his name became known throughout the nation. The 1996 branch of Netsuretsu Shokudo was located on the restaurant floor of Osaka's HEP NAVIO mall and as such was not best placed to attract Osaka's gourmets. So the idea was to create an impact and give them something to talk about. Given the constraints of the tiny budget, Morita decided to go with woks as the object most typically associated with Chinese cuisine. He hit on the idea of covering the walls with them, and this direct mode of expression resulted in a striking interior. Once the restaurant opened, you would see children taking delight in the woks on the wall at one table, while a couple would be out on a date at another; it was the décor as much as the food that was raved about.

Similarly, for each new job, Morita explains that he looks to uncover the high fashion in a structure. "Even if you're in the same building but on a different floor, conditions change. No two spaces are the same, and my job is to create a haute couture interior." Morita first takes into consideration average customer expenditure and other requirements (such as whether the restaurant will be frequented by families, couples, or people on expense accounts), then thinks up a variety of options and ways to orchestrate some drama in the space. He then carries out a simulation of the customers' movement around the space: how they walk through it, whether the corridor revealed when the door is opened seems too long, and so on. Having come up with a large number of different ideas, he considers them from the point of view of a variety of contingencies, gradually combining them to come up with a final proposal. Then, and only then, does he pick up a pen and start to draw. "I've had to come up with so many different scenarios that, in my head, I've been on a date with pretty much every supermodel there is," he laughs. Out of his animal-motif bag, the designer pulls a PC-substitute, his Sony Playstation portable, onto which he has downloaded hundreds of images of recent works. These turn out to consist not only of commercial interiors, but a wide variety of different genres such as housing, college cafeterias, stations, and communal areas in large-scale facilities. He's also been known to turn his hand to condo interiors. For him, spaces are divided into houses, which should be imbued with warmth, and commercial facilities, which should be exciting.

Morita believes that artists are free to create what they want to, as opposed to designers, whose ultimate mission is to return a profit and increase net income on each project. In the future, he plans to expand into designing products, jewelry, bags, denims and everyday goods. "Whether we're talking about toilet paper, tissue, or cotton swabs, there ought to be more everyday goods whose quality of design is what makes you want them. Even old people's homes and gravestones should be stylish!" he jokes. Spending a large part of each year overseas, the designer loves hotels and always wanted to design a five-star hotel before he hit his fortieth birthday. In 2006, this dream came true when he became involved a project for W Hong Kong, a five-star hotel operated by the Starwood group. From the banquet hall to the guest rooms, taking in the lobby, elevator hall and corridors, Morita is masterminding every detail of the interior.

Keifuku Arashiyama Station

Ukyo-ku, Kyoto / 2002

O.M.CORPORATION

Office / Nishi-ku, Osaka / 2006

08/

FANTASTIC DESIGN WORKS

Katsunori Suzuki

In a certain sense, designers can be likened to actors. Whatever the role, there are two types of actor: those who project themselves through that role; and those who, each time, completely suppress their own self to become the part they are playing. The relationship between a designer and his work is similar. Katsunori Suzuki, for example, belongs without a doubt to the latter category. Each project is imprinted with a different style, making it impossible to summarize his oeuvre in a few simple words.

Although an overwhelming proportion of his work involves restaurant and bar design, with a slew of commissions completed for overseas clients, each piece has its own distinctive style. One example that represents the diversity of

his work is the J-POP Cafe chain, in which mysterious forms and unique organic curves are blended with a sixties-style look and vivid color scheme. Falling into the *izakaya* (Japanese-style pub) category, ZARU could be a cafeteria in a city of the future. Other designs range from sophisticated restaurants offering authentic Japanese cuisine to kitschy, humorous designs for restaurants themed on vampires and Japanese fairytales. Throughout, the opulent, bewitching atmospheres he creates hark back to Japan's bubble years that so influenced his approach.

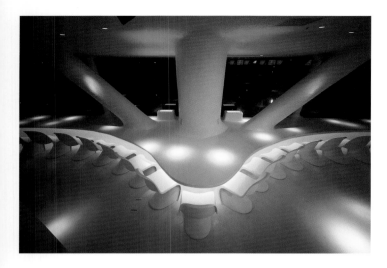

J-POP Cafe Odaiba

Restaurant /Minato-ku, Tokyo / 2002

J-POP Cafe Taipei

Restaurant /Taipei, Taiwan / 2002

Alux

Lounge and dining bar / Minato-ku, Tokyo / 2006

Blue Lounge Ryugu

Bar / Toshima-ku, Tokyo / 2005

Gorgeous & Gothic Dining, The Wizard of The Opera

Dining bar / Toshima-ku, Tokyo / 2005

Story

When Katsunori Suzuki was 19 and studying oil painting in college, he took a solo trip to New York. Walking through the streets of Manhattan, he was stopped in his tracks by Café Iguana. The thing that caught his attention was a crystal chandelier in the shape of an iguana, suspended from the ceiling at the far end of the space. In the middle of taking photos, he was interrupted by the owner of the café who'd stepped outside for a minute. As soon as she found out he was Japanese, she began recounting her plans to open a Japanese restaurant and asked him if he could come up with any interesting ideas for it. At that point, only the restaurant name —Le Bar Bat— had been decided and she was wondering what to do with the interior. Gifted at drawing, Suzuki sketched out some possibilities using bats, graveyards, churches, and so on. The owner was thrilled when he showed them to her. "Up until then, I had no idea that a restaurant could be put together like that and got to thinking that, in a place like New York, interiors could be decided on in that way."

Towards the end of his studies, Suzuki starting to think about what direction his career might take. He soon realized that a qualification in fine art could only lead to a job as an art teacher. This was at the height of the bubble years, and Suzuki often used to go out clubbing. "Clubs and discos are places where people get together, places that give birth to new encounters and human interaction. I used to like people-watching but, rather than wanting to run my own place, I was drawn to the idea of designing restaurants and bars."

Determined to find himself an apprenticeship, he moved to Tokyo and joined the MD, a design firm renowned in the industry for creating the massive nightclubs Maharaja and Area, which were two of his favorite hangouts. After a year of working for the company he happened to be leafing through a magazine that profiled overseas commercial facilities and came across an extensive review of Le Bar Bat. The owner was Joyce Steins, who had become known in the design world when her café Iguana had become a hit. "I was bowled over to see the interior that was based on my proposals. It hit me again how interesting this job was and I became even more passionate about my work." Suzuki worked his way up for 12 more years before going it alone.

Of the work Suzuki undertakes now, 90 percent consists of designs for various restaurants and bars, many of which also feature his own business ideas. He is very much into food and can often be seen going places with some new snack in hand. "Although cuisine is usually classified according to country, I think it's interesting to split it by era too. Taking things that little step further is essential. For example, *manzai* comedians constantly have to think about new material; they're not doing their job if they don't have a new way to make people laugh whenever they crash and burn."

The designer believes that commercial establishments are stage settings, tools by which proprietors earn money. "My designs can be recognized from the fact they're filled with seating, because squeezing in just one more seat has an effect on profits. Design is not just about getting people to come in and try the place out; you also need to create an appeal that will keep them happy during their drinks or meal and have them coming back for more."

Apparently, movies are a rich source of inspiration when Suzuki is together a design. For example, when he was working on J-Pop Cafe's Odaiba branch, *2001 Space Odyssey* came to mind. The interior features a large number of organic forms that resemble gigantic mollusks, while both the window-side seating and interior as a whole have touches of retro spaceships about them.

Similarities can be drawn between Suzuki's approach to design and painting a work of art. "For sketches, you first rough out the picture as a whole, before gradually filling in the details." When working on an interior, he starts by drawing a large plan, and then brings his focus down as he goes. "First, I decide the form, then move onto the colors." He believes that it is important for an interior designer to get the most out of the white box, or space, which the project will occupy. He tries to develop proposals in a straightforward way. "If you prioritize what you want to do in your designs, it's bound to unravel somewhere along the line and you'll end up with a design that feels artificial."

Suzuki may have a background in fine art but, as a designer, he makes a clear distinction between his work and that of an artist.

09/

cafe co.

Yoshiyuki Morii

Yoshiyuki Morii led the café and restaurant boom of the Nineties and has stayed at the forefront of interior design ever since, producing cutting-edge works that put him in the spotlight time and again. It's impossible to calculate how many times this designer's works have hit the design world's front pages, while a non-stop stream of commissions for commercial complexes of all shapes and sizes, including cafés, restaurants, boutiques, housing, and wedding facilities floods into his office. The proprietor of a café himself, Morii creates designs that *go* beyond considerations of mere appearance since they are based on an intuitive feel for marketing and management, backed up by experience.

The designer's mind for business, as well as his frequent, skillful use of natural elements, may well be connected to his roots. Born in Kyoto's traditional Muromachi district to a haberdasher dealing in luxury fabrics for wealthy clients, Morii is shy, yet mischievous. After spending his college years engrossed in part-time work in the restaurant business, he took two trips to America that would prove critical in determining his life path. While the designer may have taken an unconventional route to reach his current position, these experiences laid the foundations for his current work.

K-two Aoyama

K-two Aoyama

Beauty salon / Minato-ku, Tokyo / 2004

M Residence

Private residence / Kobe City, Hyogo Prefecture / 2004

Bishoku MAIMON Umeda

Japanese restaurant / Kita-ku, Osaka / 2004

Ristorante Versare

Wedding hall / Kusatsu City, Shiga Prefecture / 2005

Maison de Comtesse

Beauty salon / Chuo-ku, Osaka / 2005

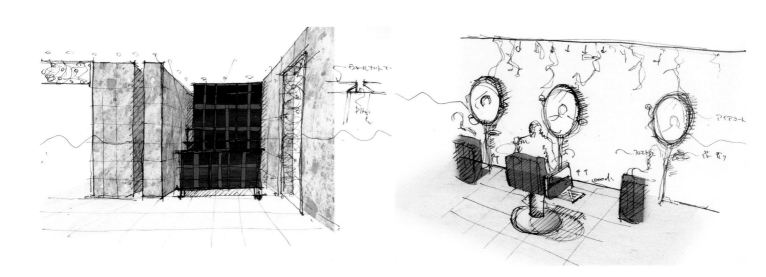

danceteria SAZA*E

Club / Kita-ku, Osaka / 2005

Tab Device Aoyama

Boutique / Minato-ku, Tokyo / 2004

Story

America is a country that has powerful connections to the life and career of Yoshiyuki Morii. The first time he visited was in 1987, when he was 20. At the time, he was studying in the Department of Architectural Design at Kyoto Junior College of Art (now Kyoto University of Art and Design) during the day, and spending every night at his job as the manager of a snack bar in Gion, Kyoto's entertainment district. Working his way up from pot-scrubber, he eventually learned everything about working in the kitchens, but his grades suffered as a result. In despair, he dropped out and headed for America, where he spent several months traveling around the Los Angeles area.

Morii wonders whether, after being brought up in the most traditional quarter of historic Kyoto, he didn't always yearn for a place that was completely different. "The environment I grew up in was set out in a neat grid like the lines on a *Go* board; even the sky was parcelled up in intersecting lines. When you looked towards the horizon, it was sliced up off by the skyline and there was no feeling of wide-open skies." What struck him in America were the wide horizons where you could feel a sense of space, completely unlike the chinks of sky seen in Kyoto.

On his return to Japan, he began work for a design office that also acted as a realtor. Though the office was doing well, riding on the bubble economy, Morii soon realized that the work was not for him and quit a year later to go back to the States. This time he went as part of a group of eight other guys calling themselves the "cheeky team." The plan was to do a coast-to-coast trip, but gradually the team members fell away until there were only three of them left. This time around, for some reason Morii found himself drawn to

architecture and urban landscapes, particularly the scenery of Manhattan that he was seeing for the first time. For the designer, it was a kind of "whopping great Kyoto," with the same vivid contrast of light and shade, and grid-like organization of the streets.

When he came back to Japan after this trip, Morii put serious consideration into his future. The father of one of his travel companions was involved in interior design projects in Osaka and Tokyo, and Morii joined the Osaka office. This was around the time that foreign architects were really starting to make their mark on Japan's landscape. Though projects such as Shigeru Uchida and Aldo Rossi's Hotel Il Palazzo, and other works by Nigel Coates inspired Morii, he still hadn't hit upon the idea of becoming a designer himself, and instead threw himself into the job he was doing.

One year later, in 1990, it was decided that he would spend several months training in the States. His destination: Columbus, Ohio. Each month, he was also responsible for visiting two other cities in order to research shopping malls. In Columbus, he lived in German Village, a district full of design offices. His interest in design growing, Morii bought book after book, touring around to seek out architecture and interiors. In Los Angeles, he fell in love with the work of Eric Owen Moss. The number of Japanese creators operating overseas was also on the increase, and pieces by Arata Isozaki were appearing on the West Coast.

The designer felt he had finally found what he was looking for in an interior when he came across Angeli in Melrose and Santa Monica's Wilshire Restaurant. Designed by Thomas Schoos, Wilshire's interior was incredibly modern; the restaurant was known at the time as a stylish place to dine out, and remains popular even today. The menu and interior form a harmony complemented by scrupulously attentive service. Perhaps Morii's style of restaurant

design has its origin here?

As he carried on working at his job, the urge to create welled up little by little until, at the age of 27, he established Unit, completed a one-off design for a chair, and took part in a gallery exhibition. A year later, he set himself up independently, opening a café and office adjacent to each other in Osaka's Minami-horie district. This was long before Starbucks had made it to Japan and his choice to locate his office next to the espresso bar was a tactical move. At work, he constantly keeps the needs of the owner in mind, even over such details as light bulbs: once he chose lighting based on the fact the bulbs were sold at the nearby convenience store.

The pieces that really launched him on the scene were the restaurant Africa and Shinobu-tei, precursors of Japan's restaurant boom. Until that point, the designer had chiefly worked on small-scale sites of 70 to 1000 square feet; he now found himself responsible for projects measuring 3500 square feet or more.

"My work style has changed over the last two years," he says. He is extremely conscious of the way his own personality comes out in his work. Orchestrating the ambience of a space, he works in collaboration with other artists, to ensure that his touch doesn't overwhelm the whole. Thus, while jettisoning a purely common-sense way of looking at things, it is vital to combine the eye of a proprietor with the tastes of a man on the street. Balancing these two contradictory aspects is what stimulates his artistic sensitivities, spurring him on to his next challenge.

10/
CURIOSITY
Gwenael Nicolas

In day-to-day life in Japan, you are almost certain to come across items designed by Gwenael Nicolas; from the logo for telecom company au to GAMEBOY; from mineral water bottles to packaging for cosmetics; from car navigation systems to plasma TVs. Take any of his product designs, particularly his containers for cosmetics, and you can rapidly gauge the particular characteristics of his look: translucency, emotional coloring, and attractive forms. It is only when you come to use his products, however, that you realize these designs are not just about superficial beauty, but that considerable thought has also gone into their functionality. According to his philosophy, note must also be taken of the physical presence of the products, as well as their interface with their surroundings. Thus, Gwenael makes us appreciate anew the philosophical truth that form is never an abstract concept, but an integral aspect of the materials, and that a tool is nothing without its user.

After majoring in interior design at E.S.A.G. School of Art in Paris, Nicolas spent some time at London's Royal College of Art, where he studied industrial design. Discovering a design magazine's special edition on Japan, he found himself drawn to the East. After arriving in Japan, Nicolas set up a company with Japanese partner Reiko Miyamoto, but his interest in the country was far removed from the Western fascination with the Orient exhibited in Japonism a century and a half earlier. Instead, the designer seems to maintain an equally cool distance from both cultures, recognizing good and bad points in Japan and France and allowing both nations to creatively inform his work.

MARS THE SALON AOYAMA

Nail salon / Minato-ku, Tokyo / 2003

NISSAN 39th Tokyo Motor Show Booth

Exhibition booth / Chiba City, Chiba Prefecture / 2005

C-1

Studio and residence / Shibuya-ku, Tokyo / 2005

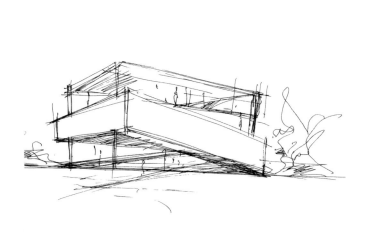

C-2

Private residence / Nishi-tsuru County,
Yamanashi Prefecture / 2006

Story

C-1, Gwenael Nicolas' home and studio, lies in a residential area in Yoyogi, Tokyo. From the outside, it resembles like a white box, and this minimal look is carried into the interior, which is a brilliant white almost entirely free of adornment. Above the first-floor studio are his private rooms, in which large windows bring light flooding into every room. In the third floor living room, Nicolas, his lean frame clothed in his preferred uniform of black turtleneck and pants, pulls a book off a shelf and settles himself on the sofa he designed. The book is *Museum Watching*, a collection of photographs by Elliott Erwitt, a photojournalist with internationally renowned cooperative Magnum Photos. It contains a selection of chance compositions shot in museums, each one a witty take on the subtle relationship between the works on exhibition and their audience. Nicolas turns the pages and stops at a picture of a female nude poised to fire her arrow into the back of a distant figure of a man disappearing down the gallery.

"The positional relationship between the humans and the works is interesting, don't you think?" comments Nicolas on the book, one of his favorites. He believes that design is not the end-result of a process. Instead, since he sees design as ultimately being fixed within the relationship between the designed object and the user; the important thing is not the object itself, but the relationship between a person and that object. Accordingly, he places great emphasis on the interface and communicative function.

To describe C-1 is to articulate his design philosophy. The structure consists of a steel frame enveloped by glass walls. Nicolas explains that the choice to connect the floors with a gentle incline instead of stairs came from the desire to create the antithesis of the staircase, a necessary evil that eats up so much space in diminutive Japanese homes. While conventional interiors unfold in a series of scenes as you open doors and navigate stairs, here, the slope renders the boundary between floors ambiguous, making it possible to comprehend the space as a single cohesive unit.

It is possible that the idea for his house dates from working on his design for the renovated Sony Showroom and Qualia Tokyo in Ginza's Sony Building. No sloping floors existed within the Sony Building, so Nicolas added skip floors to create different levels, paying close attention to the movement of visitors through the space. Introducing a spiral wall made of glass, he created a new tower within the existing skyscraper.

In his works, you often come across the technique of incorporating attractive visual devices into the space: oblique lines, helixes, overlaps, gaps and shearing add a twist to almost every interior. Research shows that people tend to perceive things according to stereotypes. Nicolas' designs seem to experiment with visual adventures that recall the discoveries of cognitive psychology, appealing to the senses of the people who experience them.

"Rather than creating a style, it's vital to engender a discovery," he says. "First, I elaborate a scenario and create a storyboard with people as the central focus, then I incorporate an element of discovery and unpredictability into that before starting on the design."

When he has completed something, Nicolas then proceeds to give a presentation to his partner, Reiko Miyamoto, which enables him to obtain both an objective evaluation of his work and the Japanese take on things. Nicolas has kept Tokyo as his base since arriving in Japan. He find the city captivating and feels that, unlike Paris, where it is clear to see what is fashionable and what is not, there is a chaotic dynamism to Japan's capital.

11/

Office of Ryue Nishizawa

Ryue Nishizawa

The Tokyo residence Moriyama House was legendary in the design world of Japan, even before its completion in 2005. The structure represents a milestone both in terms of architect Ryue Nishizawa's portfolio and the development of modern Japanese housing. Positioned about the site, white cubic volumes of varying shapes and sizes make up five airy residences, including one for the development's owner. While still demonstrating the preoccupations underlying his style, as developed through Weekend House (1998), House in Kamakura (2001), and Funabashi Apartment (2004), Moriyama House gives you the sense that Nishizawa has pushed his thinking one step further.

As a graduate student working part-time at Toyo Ito & Associates architects, Nishizawa was deeply impressed by Ito's ability to articulate his ideas on architecture in his own terms. Initially, Nishizawa worked under Kazuyo Sejima, who also belonged to the Ito school of thought, before establishing Sejima and Nishizawa and Associates (SANAA). They have collaborated on domestic projects such as Multimedia Workshop, Dior Omotesando, and the 21st Century Museum of Contemporary Art, Kanazawa, as well as being commissioned to carry out pieces overseas, including the Toledo Museum of Art Glass Pavilion, the Stadtheater in Almere, The Netherlands, and New York's New Museum of Contemporary Art.

Having won countless prizes in design competitions, Ryue Nishizawa can surely be counted among the world's most-watched architects. Assimilating their buildings into the surrounding environment, SANAA produces pared-down structures that have a translucent feel to them.

While, in a way, Nishizawa's works attest to a powerful artistic inclination, they are never purely aesthetic. Each demonstrates an improvisational approach based on a series of logical propositions. "The important thing is not whether you think a work is highly polished, logically sound, or appealing to the senses, but whether you can be satisfied with it, whether you are interrogating yourself in some way," he explains.

Moriyama House >>

Funabashi Apartment

Apartment block / Funabashi City, Chiba Prefecture / 2004

Moriyama House

Private residence and apartment block / Tokyo / 2005

21st Century Museum of Contemporary Art, Kanazawa

Art museum / Kanazawa City, Ishikawa Prefecture / 2004

Dior Omotesando

Boutique / Shibuya-ku, Tokyo / 2003

EPFL Learning Center
(library, research facilities, restaurant, exhibition and event space)
Lausanne, Switzerland, completion expected 2009

Story

Against the mountainous scenery of Gunma prefecture stands Weekend House, Ryue Nishizawa's 1998 debut project. Areas of courtyard garden divide up the interior, introducing light into the space. Outside, its surroundings are bare. There is only the solitary building, motionless, enveloped in nature. "I thought it would be interesting to introduce a free-standing cube into such a bare landscape, and so created something that would have nothing around it but the natural environment," he says. The result is this remarkable work.

Created under completely opposing conditions, Funabashi Apartment, on the other hand, had considerable limits imposed on its outward appearance, making it impossible to play with the exterior. Instead, Nishizawa focused on transforming the interior living environment. "Given the restrictions, I had to consider what to do with the interior. So, compared with other projects, the proposals were oriented much more towards interior design."

The apartment block falls into the category of 25-square-meter studio apartments for college students. "In this kind of space, if you cram a lot of things into what is essentially just a bedroom, you end up with something that lacks charm. Instead, I expanded the kitchenette and bathroom, dividing the studio into three areas: a bedroom, bathroom, and kitchen area. Or, to put it another way, each studio now boasts three living spaces."

Moriyama House dates from the same period as Funabashi Apartment, but although it consists of rental apartments, not all of it is interior-oriented. "I got the feeling that not just myself but many architects were creating proposals based purely on interior elements, like automatic locks, induction heaters,

floor heating, void spaces, and maisonette-style rooms, and that outward-looking designs were few and far between," he says. Nishizawa adds that he feels that the tendency to focus all the visual wealth inside a structure, and thus neglect the exterior, is something that exists not only amongst architects, but society in general, and that urban architecture is deteriorating as a result. If, for Moriyama House, he had chosen to erect a single structure, it would have resulted in a large, unwieldy volume. By carving up and scattering this volume he generated an open structure that starts to form a continuity with the external environment.

Although it is possible to separate Nishizawa's work into that which he undertakes through SANAA and independent projects, most of their pieces are collaborative. Similarities between the architectural styles of Nishizawa and Sejima include the belief that it is vital for designers to come up with plans that extend the post-construction life of the structure, rather than prevailing methodology that terminates with the moment of construction.

Both Moriyama House and Kanazawa's 21st Century Museum of Contemporary Art exemplify how the future users of the structure will rediscover and redefine it through various proposals incorporated into the plan. For example, trees planted around each site will act to transform the environment as they grow. In its present incarnation, Moriyama House is a cluster of apartments. The designer, however, also visualized the possibility of it becoming a single residence in the future. He calculated the change in aspect that this would entail, and planned the structure accordingly. From the word go, some aspects of this unique project were given a slightly unfinished feel, and this is what helps produce its feeling of freedom and weightlessness, combined with its subtle sense of scale.

It is easy to imagine that, to realize

multiple scenes within a single structure, SANAA starts with organic lines and curves that naturally arise from the process of demarcating spaces using surfaces (walls) and axes (columns). These lines and curves are then pulled together to form a single composition: the building as a whole. Their modeling and design appears to be created from the inside out, using a form of spatial processing based on loci of movement. There is a very close resemblance between two-dimensional artistic techniques of Paul Klee and those employed in SANAA's three-dimensional structures. To borrow the words of Frank Gehry when he discussed the boundary between sculpture and architecture: the only difference is whether a piece of work has windows, i.e. possesses both an interior and exterior. Perhaps the best way to analyze SANAA's sculptural architecture is to describe the genesis of each individual structure and allow the works to speak for themselves. This is why the designers use a minimum of words when speaking about their own work.

12/

Wonderwall Inc.

Masamichi Katayama

The scene: Japan in the Nineties. Out of the chaos of the stagnant economy emerges a new wave of design, spear-headed not by those in the industry but by writers, DJs, and musicians better described as creative entrepreneurs. Their borderless activities help transform the world of fashion.

In the midst of this turmoil appears Masamichi Katayama, a man who continues to exert a huge influence on retail design. Spaceship-like interiors enveloped in the dazzling glare of fluorescent lighting; mechanical devices, limited-edition T-shirts and sneakers... the ultimate commodities born of Japan's particular brand of consumerism; each radiating a power-ful aura from its niche in the palatial showcase of Katayama's designs.

The first collection detailing the stylish interiors of Masamichi Katayama was published in Europe in 2003 and had an enormous international impact. The book not only widened global recognition of Japanese interiors as being in the vanguard of global design, both in terms of quality and quantity, but also re-imported the information back to Japan for wider domestic attention. Katayama was instrumental in taking Japanese designs to international audiences.

"In the Eighties, more and more foreign designers were coming over to Japan and creating works, but I remember thinking it was finally the turn of Japanese designers to make it in the West," says Katayama, recalling his decision to look outwards. "Having learned form western styles, I also started to question how I wanted to present my own interpretation and designs back to audiences in Europe and the States. This was one of the reasons that motivated me in creating the monograph."

100%ChocolateCafe.

Café / Chuo-ku, Tokyo / 2004

inhabitant

Boutique / Shibuya-ku, Tokyo / 2004

The Tokyo Towers,
Sea Sky Guest 49th & 50th Floors

Guest rooms / Chuo-ku, Tokyo / 2005
(Project completion expected 2008)

BAPEXCLUSIVE™

Boutique / Minato-ku, Tokyo / 2005

Stair

Restaurant and lounge / Minato-ku, Tokyo / 2005

HYSTERIC GLAMOUR
Roppongi Hills

Boutique / Minato-ku, Tokyo / 2006

OriginalFake

Shop / Minato-ku, Tokyo / 2006

Story

The year of 2004 saw the NIGO®-designed brand A Bathing Ape®'s two-story 150-metre-square store, Busy Work Shop®, open in SoHo, New York. The man responsible for the design was Masamichi Katayama. Far away in his childhood home in Okayama, a bird's-eye-view of Manhattan that his parents bought him when he was in elementary school is still pinned up on the wall of his bedroom. He cannot recall why he had asked for it back then, but he could never have imagined that a store he designed would one day open for business in this very metropolis.

Katayama's parents run a furniture shop. From a young age, he lived with his family on the top floor of a building whose first four floors were filled with heir selections. As a middle-schooled, he had no interest in music or art, but was a boy in the school baseball team dreaming of the day he would become a pro. Yet by the time he graduated, he discovered rock music, which became his entry into all things cultural. Music, fashion, and design are all connected in some way, and Katayama was into every aspect of the world of rock, including record cover designs and fashions worn by musicians. Young people of the time were also heavily influenced by images from MTV, then rocketing into popularity.

After graduating from high school, Katayama entered a design school in Osaka, majoring in interiors. During his those years, as a student, he also started to develop an interest in architecture. "Buildings like Shin Takamatsu's Kirin Plaza Osaka and Tadao Ando's bare concrete edifices were starting to go up all over the place and I was thrilled we were getting some interesting buildings in the Kansai region too," he says. Katayama's preconceptions that architecture and interior design had to be serious were gradually starting to break down. Although he didn't much like what he was learning about interiors at the school, compared to Okayama, Osaka boasted plenty of shops he was eager to check out, and it was here that he could encounter new design. "I same to realize that design was in the same line except ahead of what you really like. From that moment on, everything became much more fun and enjoyable."

In 1992, at the age of 26, Katayama co-founded H. Design Associates with two other designers, including Tsutomu Kurokawa. It was the post-bubble era and in the following five years their work was limited to a miscellany of small projects so numerous that the designer barely recalls what they got up to. "In the Eighties, cool little stores were kept open by their sponsors whether any customers walked in or not. We physically took the blow and understood that those sweet days were over."

Meanwhile, in concert with Undercover designer Jun Takahashi, NIGO® had opened his first shop Nowhere in the Ura-Harajuku area of Tokyo. When he met Katayama five years later in 1998, he was making a name for himself in the underground, but was still not recognized by the public at large. They were introduced to each other when NIGO® was doing the rounds looking for a designer to remodel his shop. Though it was a surprise to find out that his clients was four years younger that him, as they chatted, NIGO® took a sudden shine to Katayama and their collaboration was set in motion. The result was an interior leading from a space where people could wait in line to a passageway beyond that culminated in a flight of stairs leading upwards. "I experimented with all kinds of things that would normally be frowned on in design, but he loved it. I admit it must have been a tough space to use for retail, though."

Katayama went on to churn out interior

after successful interior, each subverting the conventional expectations of a store. "If the previous brand image was all white and cool, for example, I would go ahead and flood the place with a rainbow of colors. I have constantly executed these types of brand image makeovers, and that lead up to what I do now." He says those ideas may have been an important turning point for his career. "T-shirts are no more than what they are, you know, but we're talking about things that risk becoming extremely select, or whose value is grasped solely by those people who understand that value. Some designer T-shirts end up being worth hundreds of dollars each, or may even gain a value similar to that of precious gems. Which is why gather up those gray areas purposely showcased them so that they became untouchable. He claims that his witty idea of reverentially placing the T-shirts behind glass goes beyond plain irony. Stimulating each customer with the products wrapped in an aura exceeding its actual value, or additional values gained through so-called myths of charismatic fashion people, celebrities, and shop owners, Katayama materialized the scenes behind such phenomenon, connecting vies of both suppliers and shoppers. His office brims with a mouthwatering collection of goods, figures, rare Beatles memorabilia, guitars, as well as

walls generously packed with enormous shelf-fulls of books, CDs, and DVDs, but the fact that he is an avid shopper only works to his advantage.

"A guilty pleasure of mine is to contrive to make everyone appreciate how cool something is, then watch this response spread until the status of the goods goes up a notch." For Katayama, the issue of how to create a feeling of distance between the customer and the product remains an important theme in his work. "I could go as far as having the products roll around the floor. What's interesting is working out exactly what approach to take." Katayama constantly wants to surprise people. "I'm not really into devices that are overly subjective; that's not enough to reach the public. Instead, you end up with something more powerful if you use things that everyone understands, such as glass cases, or the conveyor belt from a baggage claim. I also throw in items that I didn't design myself if that can act as something provocative for the space. I guess, a common theme of most of my designs is stimulating the viewer and making them feel just a little uneasy, in a good way! Everyone has his or her own set of values. No matter what the item may be, if you really love it, you can showcase whatever you want in your own little vitrine. Designs can also come out of such quests for value.

Young people now own both expensive items and cheaper ones; they don't rank these in terms of price, but see them as of equal value. And I rate things in this way too."

One unbeatable design element that Katayama himself takes great pride in is lighting. "Light has a huge power to appeal. Since I don't want the space to give a cheap impression, including things other than lighting, I always put serious consideration into the Color Rendering Index to create the best possible look. By using the kind of light that doesn't exist in the everyday world, I try to give people a totally new experience. I feel that things like light, scent, and sound that have no physical substance are incredibly important elements in design." Katayama feels it pointless to draw lines around the definition of an interior designer. "I don't just see other interior designers as competitors, but anyone who provides people with something fun and exciting is my rival. On the other hand, I also love to work together with creators of different backgrounds, instead of trying to do every bit of the design on my own. Direction work is something that I have started doing too. But I never intend to go as far out as fashion or graphic design. " Katayama remains keen on a variety of information and instinctive feelings.

PIERRE HERMÉ PARIS

Patisserie and café / Shibuya-ku, Tokyo / 2005

START TODAY Co., Ltd.

Office / Chiba City, Chiba Prefecture / 2005

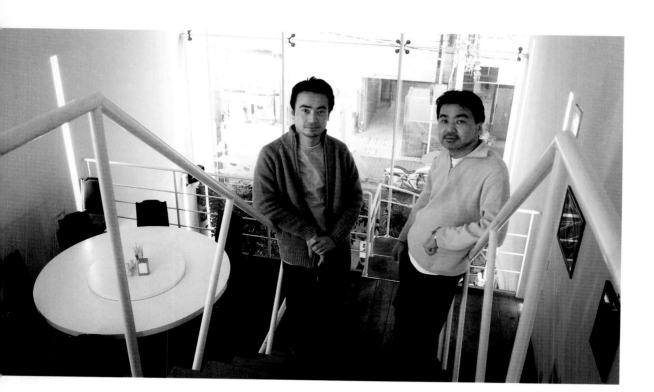

13/

Naya architects

Manabu Naya +
Arata Naya

The various guises of houses built by brothers Manabu and Arata Naya can be traced to their well-thought-out plans that focus on putting the client first. After founding their design firm, the pair cut their teeth on countless designs for shops, restaurants, and commercial facilities, and this experience has enabled them to inject their more recent interiors with a high degree of polish.

Allowing yourself to be taken in by their direct way of speaking, however, risks overlooking the originality of their work. A closer look reveals unexpectedly avant-garde details beneath the sober veneer of each design.

Their very first residential project, House in Kyouto, is notable for the radical decision not to put glass in the latticework front door, which means that fresh air constantly circulates through the interior. Elsewhere, the immense facade of Chinese restaurant HOUCHINROU seems to float into view as you walk along a Kawasaki shopping street. For the steel skeleton, where eight supporting columns would have been sufficient, the brothers chose to use 78 lengths of 10-centimeter H-section steel, which were then panelized in the factory prior to assembly. For the House in Tamagawadai, to prevent it from dominating over the surrounding environment, rooms were arranged so that they appear to exist in isolation, each slightly offset from the others; the concept was essentially a set of rooms stacked on top of each other like boxes.

House in Futakoshinchi >>

HOUCHINROU

Chinese restaurant / Kawasaki City, Kanagawa Prefecture / 2001

House in Futakoshinchi

Private residence / Kawasaki City, Kanagawa Prefecture / 2004

House in Edogawa

Private residence / Edogawa-ku, Tokyo / 2005

House in Tamagawadai

Private residence / Setagaya-ku, Tokyo / 2005

Story

"Even now, I don't think of myself as an architect," says Manabu Naya. "Sometimes I catch myself thinking: how cool it would be to become one." When asked how he does see himself, he replies, "As a designer. I think of architects as being a little more grand."

All of this is said with a straight face and no trace of irony, posturing, or self-effacement. "That's what I trained as, so when I'm introduced as an architect, I still feel a bit awkward."

Rather than leaving you with a strong impression of the architect's personality, the Naya brothers' projects instead favor a philosophy of specificity, exuding the impression that the client's lifestyle has been somehow distilled and given form.

"In terms of process, we feel that as long as the design remains our own original work, that's good enough for us," says younger brother Arata.

"We focus on the client's lifestyle and aspire to mould their way of life into some kind of form," adds Manabu. "We don't even consider how we should express ourselves through the work. Our approach consists primarily of manifesting the client in the design." He points out that there are architects whose buildings you can identify at a glance, while someone like Jean Nouvel creates buildings whose provenance cannot be so easily guessed at. "Even though it's not a specific goal, the way which we seek out solutions still generates certain common characteristics in our designs, and discovering these is an aspect of the job we both get a kick out of."

The offices of Naya architects can be found in a residential district in Kawasaki city, not far from Tokyo. A remodeled former factory, the building has shutter doors and yellow exterior walls that give it the appearance of an engineering firm. Translucent white polycarbonate panels divide the high-ceilinged steel skeleton into separate offices for the two brothers and other staff. Their desks are surrounded on three sides by piles of building materials, bookshelves and Harley Davidson Sportster 1200s.

The brothers are originally from Noshiro city in northern Japan's Akita prefecture, and both majored in architecture at the Shibaura Institute of Technology. When he was an elementary school student, Manabu was vaguely interested in civil engineering projects like dams and bridges. Engrained in his memories of that time is the experience of gazing up at what was then Japan's tallest edifice, Tokyo's World Trade Center Building, on the train out of Hamamatsucho. After graduating from college, he joined the studio of Masayuki Kurokawa, an architect who shared his approach. "At the time, Kurokawa was working in both architecture and product design. He has this spiel about how ashtrays were structures too." Later, Manabu moved on to work for Masamitsu Nozawa, an architect at the other end of the design spectrum.

Younger brother Arata was more interested in creating furniture and other objects on a more intimate scale. Thinking that if he could master architecture, he would be capable of designing objects of any size, he also chose to study architecture. On graduation, Arata was attracted to the ambiguous nature of Riken Yamamoto's work, crossing the boundary between interior and exterior, and signed up to work for him for two years.

The brothers established their current office in 1993. Their first design was Hanase, a ceramics store, and was instantly written up in an industry magazine. Before long, they began to see an increase in commissions for residential projects. "Store interior designers generally think in the short term, whereas architects are looking to create something that will last 50 or 100 years. This means we offer details and interiors that are not merely cosmetic. Conversely, for shop design you have to be incredibly meticulous and, even now, I use what I learned when we were just starting out," comments Manabu.

Seen from the world of interior design, the brothers' way of piecing together their designs using a structural approach lends a certain freshness to their store interiors, while there are many occasions where the detail-oriented, soft approach favored in interior design makes itself felt in their architecture in a way seldom seen in the industry. For example, the highly acclaimed harmonies found in their renovation projects spring from a strong awareness of interior design. As Manabu comments, "Among architects, there's still a widespread tendency to give something a hard finish and lay bare the structure, so our kind of interior-oriented design might be seen as lax by harsher critics. But if someone is capable of doing something, then why shouldn't they? I see nothing wrong with someone who isn't an architect designing something, as long as the end result is professional."

14/

C.C. DESIGN Inc.

Claudio Colucci

The sculptural furniture designed by Claudio Colucci has such a powerful presence that merely introducing it into a space transforms the whole atmosphere. In fact, in his interiors his furniture often takes on an installation-like quality that transcends its prescribed function.

Colucci's pieces include the celebrated heart-shaped chairs and the four-legged table that hints of a pet constantly on the verge of scampering off. Employing a diverse range of lines and shapes, they bring to mind all kinds of things, from plants and animals to building blocks, children's toys, mushrooms and candy, and can truly be recognized as works of art. Though on the surface his furniture has a touch of Sixties retro about it, it also radiates stability and timelessness, while brimming with humanity and pop art playfulness.

Having studied in London, Paris, and Geneva, it is hardly surprising that Colucci has become an international designer with offices in Paris and Tokyo. His discerning eye was among the first to reject the Orientalist attitude associated with Japanese art and he went on to incorporate some of its more unique aspects into his own philosophy of design.

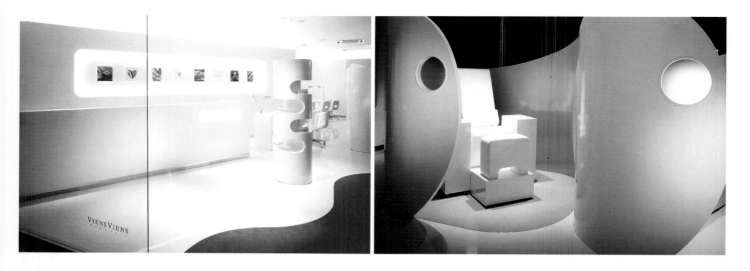

VIENS VIENS

Nail salon / Shibuya-ku, Tokyo / 2004

delicabar

Patisserie store and café / Paris, France / 2003

lafuma

Boutique / Shibuya-ku, Tokyo / 2005

Roll Madu

Café / Kita-ku, Osaka / 2004

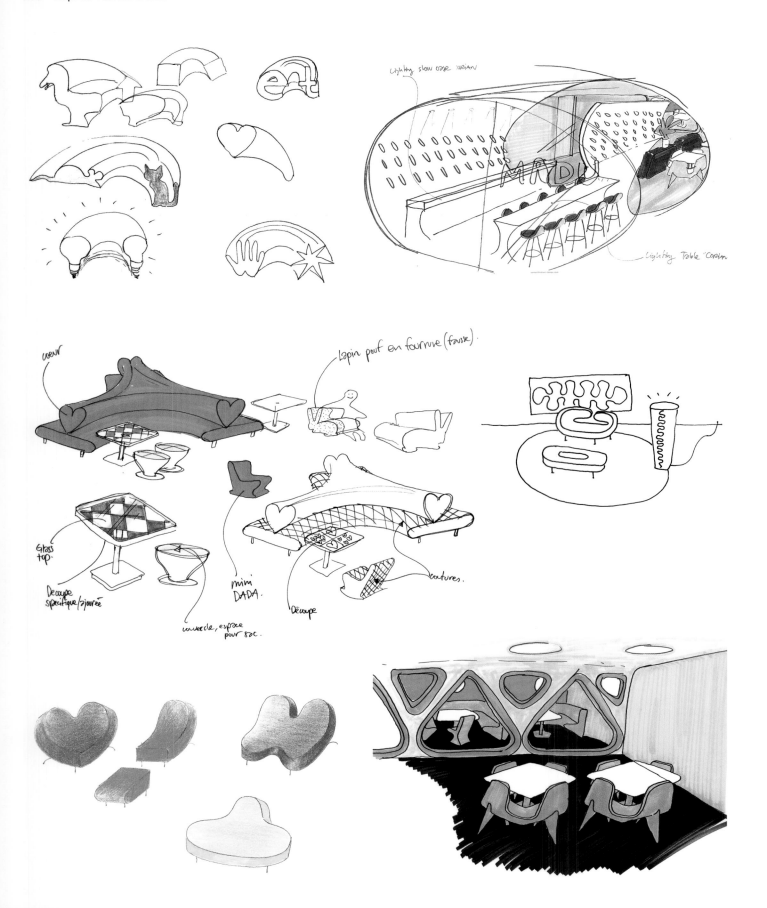

Story

Claudio Colucci's father was born on a farm near Naples in southern Italy. As soon as he graduated from high school, at the age of just 16, he headed for Switzerland with his younger brother to look for work. With no money to speak of, they elected to hitchhike; apparently it took them a whole year to arrive at their destination. During his lifetime, Colucci's father held down 40 to 50 jobs in patisserie shops, glassmakers, and design firms, before founding his own glass-related company. In his free time, he devoted himself to the practice of judo.

"He was the sensei of a judo club in Geneva, you know," says Claudio Colucci. "The fact that I also practice judo is because of him. His dream was to come to Japan with his family; he wanted to see the place where judo originated, as well as come into contact with the mind and soul of the Japanese people.

Sadly, his father was never to realize his dream, passing away at the age of just 42. "It's strange that I've ended up here instead," he says. "I never imagined I'd come to Japan and stay for such a long time."

When Colucci was six, his family moved from Locarno, near the Italian border, to Geneva. As a teenager, having graduated in graphic design at art school, he went to Paris to study industrial arts at the Ecole National Supérieure de Création Industrielle. A scholarship from the Ecole enabled him to cross the Channel and continue his studies at London's Kingston Polytechnic (now Kingston University). The internships he undertook during his time in London would prove to be extremely valuable experiences. Colucci first had the opportunity to study under Ron Arad, who was involved in new showroom and office projects at the time. Working at this office, where employees were treated as equals, proved highly rewarding.

"What I learned through this experience was that being a designer is about having the freedom to create objects for you personally." Pointing the chair he is sitting on, Colucci continues, "This piece is from the Limited Design project I'm currently working on. It's made of Corian and is something that I created solely with myself in mind. What I mean is that, rather than worrying about production lines or anything else, you just make what you want to make the way you want to make it. That's something I learned from Arad."

The second place Colucci chose to apprentice at was architect Nigel Coates' office. Coates had already won international acclaim for projects in Japan, South Africa, and the UK and Colucci was able to observe the workflow for various international projects as they were developed. What he noticed was that, by giving his staff a certain amount of freedom, Coates ended up with better results. "The way I work now can be traced back to what I learned during my internships," he concludes.

On his return to Paris, Colucci continued his studies while working part-time for Pascal Mourgue (younger brother to Olivier Mourgue, who designed the stage sets for Kubrick's *2001 Space Odyssey*). After graduation, he co-founded flexible design unit RADI DESIGNERS, at one point finding himself having dinner with Philippe Starck, and started to produce some provocative works. It was around that time that a trip to Japan was proposed by his then-girlfriend, who was studying Japanese.

The Japan of 1996 was suffering the after-effects of the economic crash and jobs were few and far between, but Colucci managed to find a position as a designer affiliated with furniture company IDEE. When his girlfriend returned to the UK, he decided to stick it out in Japan. The prevalence of superior craftsmen and wealth of technical knowledge and information were just a couple of the reasons that kept him there. After arriving in the country, Colucci became fascinated by Japanese subcultures; fired up by the teenage obsession with *kawaii* cuteness, he designed his heart-shaped furniture. This craze for *kawaii* and Harajuku-style youth fashion has recently taken the West by storm, but Colucci was the first to appreciate its worth.

15/

Klein Dytham architecture

Astrid Klein + Mark Dytham

These pieces, with their stylish look and their way of harmonizing with the landscape, would trick anyone into thinking they had been produced by Japanese designers. A closer examination, however, turns up shades of color, unique materials, and odd little twists that hint at slightly different origins. They are in fact the work of Klein Dytham architecture (KDa).

Bright and fashionable, articulate and amusing, KDa's work transcends borders to encompass architecture, interiors, furniture, and temporary structures. A world away from strict logic and formal ideologies, these pieces remind us that architecture and design exist to enhance our daily lives and surroundings. Indeed, KDa are pioneers playing a valuable role in shaking up the Japanese architectural design world with its overly formal tendencies.

Mark Dytham and Astrid Klein came to Japan in 1988 and, after two years at Toyo Ito and Associates, Architects, went on to found their own design office and produce unique concepts guaranteed to put them in the limelight.

One of them is in Yamanashi prefecture's of Kobuchizawa, where KDa has given a new lease of life to a lush resort complex overlooking the Yatsugatake mountain range. Their design for this destination is so innovative, it has garnered attention as far away as London, thus setting new projects in motion for this visionary pair.

LEAF Chapel

Chapel / Kobuchizawa, Yamanashi Prefecture / 2004

BRILLARE

Party space / Kobuchizawa, Yamanashi Prefecture / 2005

YY grill

Barbecue restaurant / Kobuchizawa, Yamanashi Prefecture / 2004

GAO

Activity center / Kobuchizawa,
Yamanashi Prefecture / 2004

BOOKS & CAFE

Café and bookstore / Kobuchizawa, Yamanashi Prefecture / 2005

UNIQLO Ginza

Boutique / Chuo-ku, Tokyo / 2005

BILLBOARD Building

Accessory shop / Minato-ku, Tokyo / 2005

HEIDI House

Residence and office / Shibuya-ku, Tokyo / 2005

Story

Despite the late hour, the basement club is abuzz with excitement. Seating around the central stage is filled to capacity, and latecomers are packed like sardines into every square inch of standing room. One after another, young people representing a plethora of nationalities take the stage to present their work, while conversations can be overheard in as many different languages. The MCs, mingling with the crowd and taking turns with the microphone, are Astrid Klein and Astrid Mark Dytham. Mixing fluent Japanese with the Queen's English, they fire up the audience and keep the event moving. The location is SuperDeluxe, a club in Tokyo's Nishi-Azabu; the event is their monthly Pecha Kucha Night, born when Mark and Astrid invited the creative people they knew to a spontaneous event for them to showcase their activities, regardless of genre. More than a few of the young participants fly in from abroad specifically to attend the event.

"There is nowhere for creative young people to exhibit their work. If you're not famous, then no magazine will even consider reviewing you. We thought it would be good to have some kind of impromptu session where creative people could meet up with friends, have fun and network in a more relaxed setting," explains Klein.

Pecha Kucha Night is an important element of KDa's activities, and one that they invest a lot of energy in. It has recently gone global, with events now being held in cities as far apart as London, Rotterdam, Shanghai, San Francisco, Berlin, and Glasgow, to name a few.

Astrid Klein was born in Varese, Italy, to a father who was the only one out of four children to not become an artist. Instead, he studied science, found a job connected with the implementation of atomic energy, and helped support his siblings. From around the age of 18, Klein herself became interested in art, and initially elected to study interior design. Later, she decided to branch out into architecture and entered London's Royal College of Art (RCA). Having lived all her life in Europe, Japan held great attraction for her. Iit seemed incredibly exotic, a country where all kinds of interesting things existed side by side. Added to this was the fact that Japan was at the height of the bubble economy and scores of Western architects and designers were being invited over to work on projects. A flood of articles in UK magazines featuring unique structures by people like Masaharu Takasaki, Atsushi Kitagawara, and Makoto Watanabe sparked her imagination. "For young designers and architects seeing these things from conservative Europe, Japan seemed like a country where anything was possible." So, along with Mark Dytham, whom she'd met at the RCA, Astrid took the plunge and booked her flight to Japan.

Mark Dytham was brought up in Milton Keynes, the first of the UK's planned communities known as New Towns. Located about 35 minutes out of London by train, the city houses a quarter of a million people in 42 square miles, or an area slightly larger than that contained within Tokyo's Yamanote train loop. It was the world's first designated New Town and Dytham watched the city develop as he grew up. He became interested in modern urban landscapes and architecture and was enamored with the idea of becoming an architect from a young age. Following his mother's advice, he applied for a part-time post in the Milton Keynes Development Corporation, working in the architecture department from the age of 16 to 18. "They were kind enough to put me in charge of projects. Only small facilities like shelters at the cricket ground, that kind of thing." Having picked up a fair amount of practical skills at a young age, he went on to graduate top of his class at university.

Since coming to Japan, the duo have been constantly stimulated and inspired by the country, and continue to produce intriguing designs that pique the curiosity. A pair of tricksters, they have revitalized Japanese architecture and design, communicating their exploits to the rest of the world. Dytham, citing the example of Honda re-importing their large-scale bikes, comments, "We're now being re-imported too." They have no intention of founding an office in London, nor of leaving their base in Tokyo.

The pair feel that Japanese urban landscapes generally come across as impersonal, but Toyo Ito's works, for example, always have that "surprise factor," a greater energy than most works produced by younger designers, as well as a spirit of endeavor which everyone can relate to. "Rather than always walking the well-trodden path the same way as everyone else, I want to go in my own direction, trying new things as I go. It's true of anything that if you don't try something, you won't know if you can do it," says Dytham. "If you find something interesting, then it's worth your while to do. The best product you can work on is your own life," Klein adds. Their dream is to continue to take on new challenges even after retirement.

16/

Hitoshi Abe

For Miyagi Stadium, one of Hitoshi Abe's best-known works, the designer integrated the structure into the surrounding hillside, subverting the closed-off, imposing characteristics that typify stadium buildings by opening it up to the exterior. After studying the contours of the location and normal geometry of a stadium, he went against the trend for a stack of concentric rings, and instead created a series of overlapping circles centered on different points to fuse the building with the landscape. For another project, KAP, rather than being parceled up into individual rooms according to purpose, this design consists of a single flexible box. Yet another work saw the creation of an additional interior wall in steel paneling, allowing the designer to link the first and second floors of the restaurant Aoba-tei in AIP. This surface was punched with tiny holes in a pixilated image of nearby zelkova trees and then backlit to generate the effect of sunlight filtering through their branches.

Rather than focusing purely on the conditions of the site, Hitoshi Abe unearths rules previously hidden beneath the surface to not only redefine the building itself, and its purpose, but also create structures with completely new functionality.

SBP

Bridge / Shiroishi City, Miyagi Prefecture / 1994

KAP

Assembly hall / Amakusa County, Kumamoto Prefecture / 2002

AIP

Restaurant / Sendai City, Miyagi Prefecture / 2005

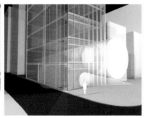

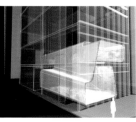

SSM

Museum / Shiogama City, Miyagi Prefecture / 2005

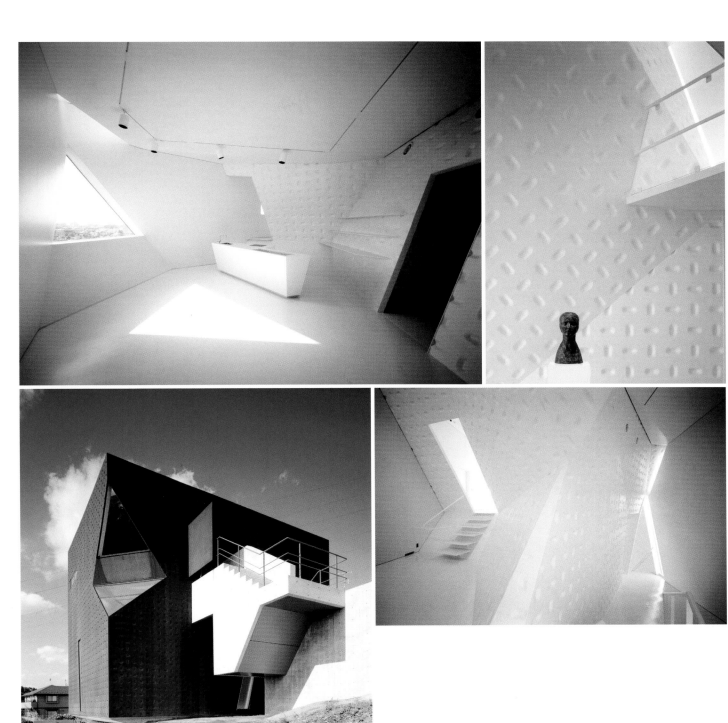

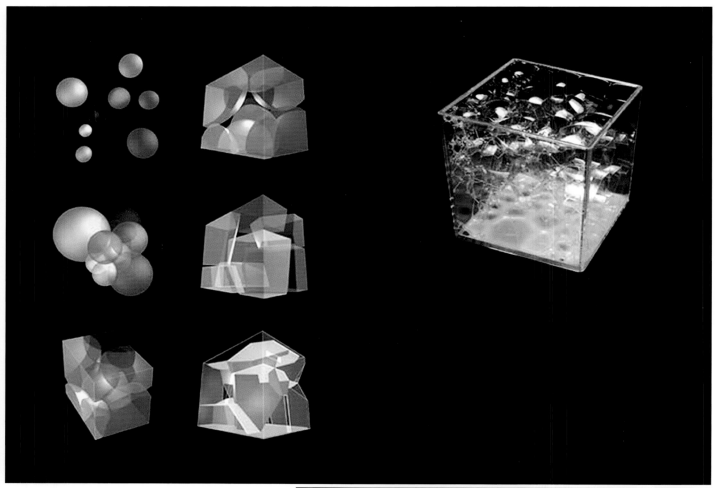

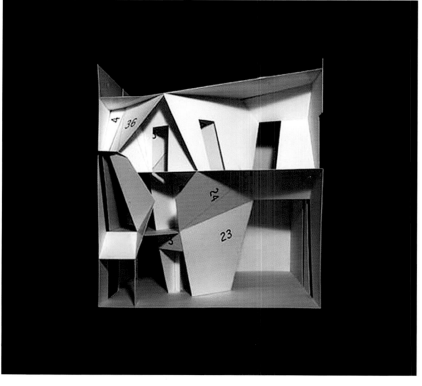

SSM concept model

Story

"While I'm not denying individual authorship, I've chosen to reject the architectural style that constantly comes to the forefront of the design, in favor of creating structures that interpolate themselves more delicately into the site and surrounding environment, resulting in buildings that dominate the site," says Hitoshi Abe.

Since this connectedness implies the relationships between a number of disparate bodies, the architect often employs the word "boundary" when talking about his work, citing as a model the planes created between soap bubbles when they cling together. Each individual soap bubble is defined by these boundaries and its interrelationships with the other bubbles. What Abe is aiming for is to embody these fluid demarcations in his works.

"Drawing the boundary between things is one of the most fundamental acts of architecture," he says.

In 1985, after graduating from Tohoku University, Abe moved to the United States to study at the Southern California Institute of Architecture (SCI-Arc) and assist at Coop Himmelblau's Los Angeles office. Before crossing the Pacific, Abe had been questioning the buildings that were materializing in architecture and seeking his own methodology. At SCI-Arc, he had the chance to attend lectures by the president of Coop Himmelblau, Wolf Prix, who also happened to become his advisor. His old image of architecture was rapidly being worn down and he was being greatly influenced Prix's take on architecture. On completion of his MA in 1988, Abe spent four years working at Coop Himmelblau, before retuning to Japan in 1992 and setting up his own company.

SSM, Abe's design for Kanno Museum, was modeled on the behavior of soap bubbles. This versatile structure consists of exhibition spaces for sculptures by eight artists, including Rodin, Moore, Manzu, Faccini, and Despiau, housed in a cube-like exterior constructed from Cor-ten steel. "The normal, layered model of architecture has to contain absolute coordinates in it somewhere, and these end up dictating the positions and types of space found on each floor," he explains. "Using the soap bubble model, the whole is decided from the relationships between its individual parts, thus preserving their identities through their respective sizes and positions." Although exhibiting artworks in white cubes while confining more playful designs to communal areas might be seen as the most appropriate way of designing an art museum, Abe took into account the fact that this building would house small sculptures in a permanent exhibition, and so pursued the image of a temple where art and gallery could become one. "Rather than placing the sculptures in an empty box of a space, I decided to build a unique design in which art and structure become interdependent," he says. Steel panels were stamped into shape and welded together in a honeycomb construction configured from the requirements of the space to create the individual soap bubble cells. Each elliptical dimple in the surfaces measures 15 centimeters by 7 centimeters. Instead of the conventional plain paint finish, these surfaces were left slightly rough, adding to their sculptural quality.

Not far from Shiroishi station on the JR Tohoku Honsen line, in Miyagi prefecture's Shiroishi city, a strangely shaped bridge spans the narrow Saikawa river. Erected in 1994 as part of economic development initiatives by Shiroishi city, the reincarnated bridge was designed to be the symbol of the city. Although, chronologically, plans for Miyagi stadium preceded this project, the bridge was the first work to be completed after Abe established his own business, and provides a fine example of his way of looking at things as an architect. Confronted with numerous standards and regulations concerning load, height, and such, when talking designs through with a public works consultant, Abe chose to turn the concept on its head. "If everything has to be based on rules, then how about giving those rules physical form?" he muses. "Geographical features are created through organic activity and then assigned a significance by man; if you give form to the invisible rules that govern things, and bring out the beauty of these rules, there will always be someone who seizes on it as some kind of metaphor." When you drive over his bridge, it seems to undulate like the images in a flipbook. Even the name, Shirasagi Bashi (Bridge of the Snowy Egret) comes from its dynamic resemblance to the rhythm of the bird's beating wings.

Abe is not the type of person to impose his particular approach on a project and then pass it over to a consultant. Since each individual project is met with experimentation, there is clear evidence in his work of a variety of directions and solutions, resulting in some vastly different structures.

17/

FUMITA DESIGN OFFICE INC.

Akihito Fumita

Like any work of art, Akihito Fumita's interiors possess a compelling individuality. In each piece, the entire space seems to have been taken over by an immense installation, making it feel as though you are entering another world when you step inside. Hiroshima boutique, ANAYI, for example, appears to have been constructed out of individual wooden blocks to form a complex 3D puzzle. Its interlocking elements seem to have been momentarily frozen at the very instant they came together to form the space, and you can imagine them gently floating off in all directions.

Fumita conceives of light as having substance, to be used like any other material. Rather than simply reflecting light or directing it onto objects, he employs it as a further component of the design. In household appliance showroom SPIRITUAL MODE, this idea has been taken one step further: rather than being formed out of the usual sections of wood and metal, it appears to be sculpted purely out of light. Elsewhere, apparel showroom m-i-d press features 400 glowing objects that bring to mind nuclear reactor cores; these generate luminous dashed lines, multiplied in mirrored surfaces so they appear to be floating in midair. The space doesn't have the chilly ambiance you might expect, but is dominated by the presence of these strange objects and their mysterious luminescent aura.

SPIRITUAL MODE >>

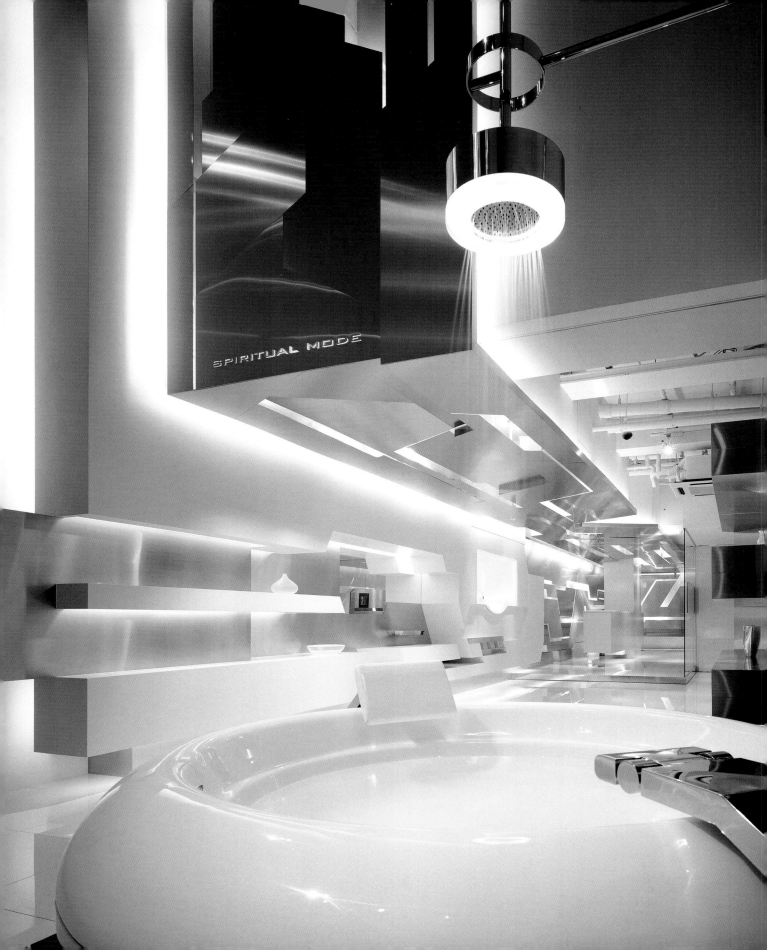

NISSAN GALLERY GINZA

Car showroom / Chuo-ku, Tokyo / 2001

m-i-d press

Apparel showroom and Tokyo office /
Shibuya-ku, Tokyo / 2004

H-House

Private residence / Shibuya-ku, Tokyo / 2004

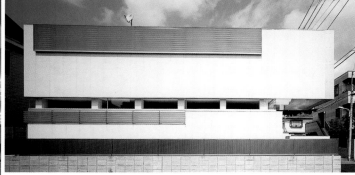

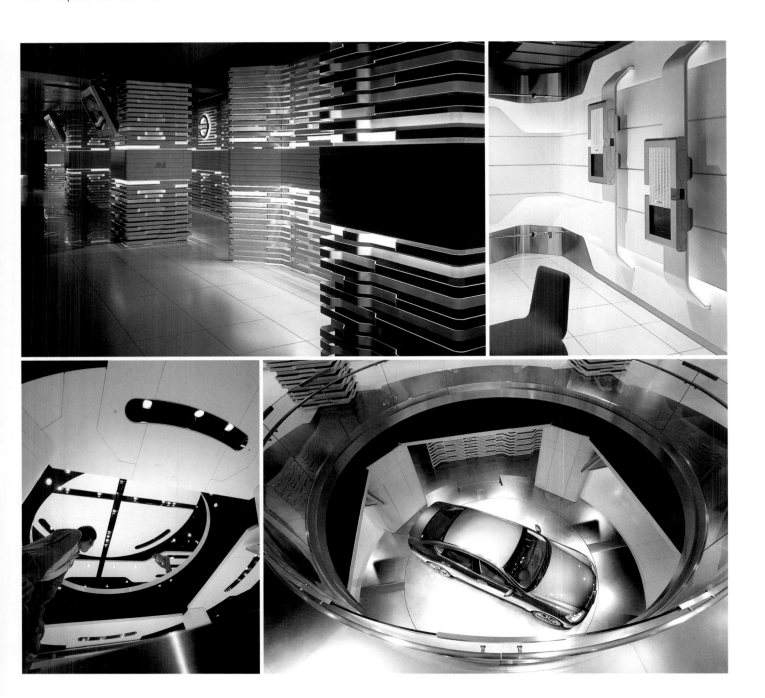

NISSAN GALLERY SAPPORO

Car showroom / Sapporo City, Hokkaido / 2004

ANAYI (Hiroshima Fukuya Ekimae)

Boutique / Hiroshima City, Hiroshima Prefecture / 2005

SPIRITUAL MODE

Household appliance showroom / Minato-ku, Tokyo/2005

Story

The extension of Akihito Fumita's fame beyond the confines of the design industry can perhaps be attributed primarily to his work on car showrooms. In 2001, he was responsible for NISSAN's gallery and main showroom in Tokyo's affluent Ginza district, creating a futuristic, cool interior filled with white light, like the inside of a spaceship. Traditionally, the automobile industry has opted for stereotypically conventional facilities: showrooms tend to be un-individuated spaces where the only defining feature is an expanse of glass in the façade.

In 1993, however, Toyota enlisted the services of theatrical designer Seno Kappa and interior designer Yasuo Kondo, and subsequently caused a sensation in 1993 when it opened its epoch-making Amlux showroom (now closed) in Umeda, Osaka. The decade also saw NISSAN start to reorganize its sales network, redesigning both its products and business environment, and entrusting Fumita with the remodeling of its showrooms.

"At the time, it wasn't just their showrooms, but the entire virtual identity of the company that needed tightening up," he explains. "To give an example, even the company's logo varied from country to country and region to region. Neither was the company making the best of its Ginza Yon Chome showroom. The time had come for them to reexamine those problems."

Until that point, NISSAN had commissioned a number of different creators to work on different issues, but now they began to feel the need for a partner who could grow with the company.

It was in 2001 that Fumita handed Nissan their new showroom. Although they had already met at various presentations Fumita admits to feeling no small amount of trepidation when NISSAN's newly elected CEO Carlos Ghosn appeared on the scene to give the showroom a final once-over before the launch. It was common knowledge that Ghosn believed design strategy to be one of the most important themes in his quest to turn the company around. After a quick glance around the space, he looked at Fumita and announced, "Good job!"

For the next three years, Fumita was responsible for NISSAN's three showrooms in Fukuoka, Nagoya and Sapporo, as well as booth design for various motor shows. In the process, he gained international recognition for the originality of his work.

Fumita's first interior after going solo in 1995 was for the beauty salon K-two. In reaction to the collapse of the bubble economy, it had become the accepted style merely to position furniture within a simple space. Fumita, however, was taken with the novel effects that lighting design and light effects could produce. Lighting becomes highly effective in plain, white-painted spaces and the designer chose to employ a variety of light effects to increase the drama of the space. The following year, budgetary restrictions came into play in the design for relaxation space NATURAL BODY. In response, Fumita came up with a curiously shaped massage treatment chair that has hints of both rabbit and robot about it. Here, the theme of relaxation is not expressed using a tangible motif, but simply through abstract light effects and the form of this distinctive chair.

Originally, Fumita had stronger leanings towards becoming an architect. During his college years, he apparently devoured architectural publications and his preconceptions that architecture was about formal equations involving math, physics, and purely practical issues began to fall away. He realized that he would be able to create the spaces he wanted to whether he became an architect or a designer. One book he was particularly influenced by was *The Architecture of the Jumping Universe* by Charles Jencks. "I get the feeling that when Japanese designers attempt to create something postmodern, it only works on a superficial level." He became fascinated by deconstruction and started to interpret it and allow it to inform his work in his own inimitable style. While still working for a design office, he oversaw a project for a station building called Tennoji MIO and choose to use deconstructivist concepts in the design.

Fumita is also attracted to cutting-edge Western architecture, but manages to avoid creating designs that reduce what he sees to an empty Japanese-style reproduction. "Since Japanese architectural design is not bound to the same conventions as Western architecture, Europeans might see it as being very free. But in reality, not only is it a disadvantage for us to have no recent tradition on which to base things, but it also makes it harder to fit things into ongoing Japanese conventions." Fumita sought to incorporate some Japanese elements into the design for NISSAN's gallery without allowing them to destroy his own style, which is strongly characterized by freedom of interpretation and a high degree of abstraction.

NATURAL BODY NAMBA CITY
Relaxation salon / Chuo-ku, Osaka / 1996

18/

Hashimoto Yukio Design Studio Inc.

Yukio Hashimoto

Yukio Hashimoto is drawn to things imbued with history and tradition. As a student, one sight that had the strongest effect on him was Taian, the miniature tearoom of 16th century tea master Sen no Rikyu, located in the grounds of Myokian Temple, Kyoto. What he liked about the tearoom was the delicate way in which an avant-garde style had been condensed into the tiny space. He also had the impression he was looking at hyper art in the traditional design of gardens in Shanghai, and detecting a purpose based on a macrocosm of the eye of God in the designs of various landscape designers and architects.

Hashimoto has been known to distinguish between these and contemporary styles, and reference them in his work. His designs pay witness to his ability to unearth an inexhaustible supply of inspiration slumbering in things usually regarded as old-fashioned, and reviving them as progressive or avant-garde. Perhaps thanks to a childhood enveloped in abundant natural surroundings, full of water and greenery, Hashimoto frequently employs natural motifs into his work. Using steel, glass, mirrors, acrylic, and textiles he manages to imbue his interiors with natural elements such as water, fire, rain, fog, mist, boulders, and forests. A feature of his style is his focus on the approach; in these zones, he plays with natural motifs that also seem to possess a sci-fi underbelly. Every approach leaves a powerful impression on the visitor: flowers entrapped in acrylic, steel latticework reminiscent of trees, and images of water projected onto various surfaces.

MINERVA

Club / Higashiyama-ku, Kyoto / 2004

SUIKYOTEI

Restaurant and bar / Chuo-ku, Tokyo / 2005

KAMONKA Ueno Bamboo Garden

Chinese restaurant / Taito-ku, Tokyo / 2005

I House

Private residence / Inagi City, Tokyo / 2005

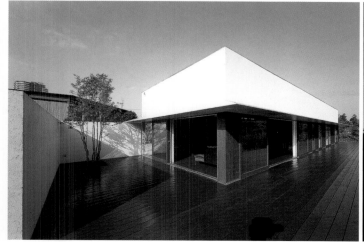

CHANTO NEW YORK

Restaurant / New York, USA / 2006

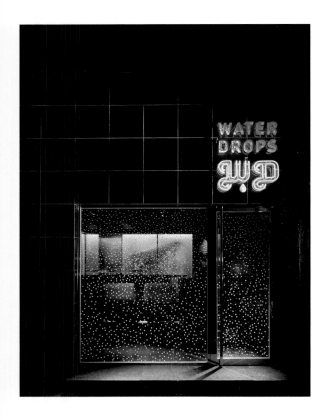

WATER DROPS

Bar / Minato-ku, Tokyo / 2006

Story

When he was first starting to think about job-hunting after college, Yukio Hashimoto couldn't come up with anything that sounded interesting. So, with the idea of talking things over with the man he revered most in the world, he got on the train to Tokyo. In a phone booth, he flipped through the pages of the phone book looking for that person's name: Shiro Kuramata. Fully expecting to get knocked back, he took the plunge and dialed and was surprised by the designer's ready acquiescence to see him.

Kuramata kindly looked over the portfolio of the young man who had called him out of the blue, and then brought over some of his own sketches. "It was like we were comparing notes on our work. And this was with a guy who I thought was the best designer in the world...!" says Hashimoto. Kuramata turned out to be extremely approachable, bringing Yukio a soda and talking to him as though to a friend. What made the strongest impression on the student was Kuramata's comparison of Eastern and Western architectural design. "He asked me what I thought the differences were between interiors in the East and West, and when I replied 'Well, one thing is the use of materials like stone and paper,' he countered that, although there was that too, he saw it as the difference between a wall and a column. He went on to explain that when a wall topples over, it can only fall in two directions, whereas you can have no idea which direction a pillar will fall in, and that this illustrated an important distinction." The two continued to discuss theories of space for some time and Yukio began to understand that, when certain key terms were used, a three-dimensional image would instantaneously appear in Kuramata's mind. "It was such a thrill to have the chance to share these 3-D images that would swell up like ideas." As a result of their talk, Hashimoto ended up doing a week-long internship at the company.

Later on, Hashimoto would spend a total of 10 years attached to the offices of SuperPotato, brainchild of another designer he looks up to as a master of the profession: Takashi Sugimoto. One of Hashimoto's most striking works of that period was SHUNJU, a restaurant located in Akasaka, Tokyo. Though the interior measured a mere 99 square meters in area, the planning stage alone is said to have taken nearly a year. For the elaborate décor, Hashimoto collaborated with ceramicists and large numbers of artisans skilled in producing traditional earthen walls and carpentry. He admits that it was this experience of working closely with creative professionals in a different field to him that first awakened in him an understanding of what design really was. "Just voicing an idea into very simple words was enough for them to generate mock-ups or produce drawings. They were able to grasp things in a very sensory way and express at a glance the quality of something like a chair, for example, and whether it was worth bothering with or not. They understood things in a very physical sense and out of this perfect collaboration was born something with the ability to move people."

After he had established himself independently, an important turning point for Hashimoto came when Osaka restaurant group CHANTO opened Daidaiya in Shinjuku. Owner-chef Kenichiro Okada, known as something of a soldier of fortune in the industry, had decided to expand into Tokyo and commissioned Hashimoto to design his second restaurant. The pair discussed how they could come up with a Japanese style like nothing anyone had ever seen before. Around that time, an up-market Japanese restaurant called Nobu was taking New York by storm, and Okada and Hashimoto gave serious thought to producing a design that would be ranked a success not only in Tokyo, or Japan, but on a global scale. The period also marked the start of a proliferation of collaborations between foreign and Japanese artists and interior designers both inside and outside the country. For this particular project Hashimoto called on UK graphic design group Tomato to help them out.

"Because I had experienced working the SuperPotato way, I think there was part of me bound to that approach, but I was also able to launch myself away from that, and have fun at the same time." In 2006, when CHANTO opened its New York debut restaurant in Greenwich Village, Hashimoto was once again placed in charge of the interior. For this piece, Hashimoto chose not to use any of the techniques he had employed in Tokyo, but instead produce an image of New York across every inch of the space. The result was an interior that gives less the impression of a make-or-break piece of fun than a distinct feeling of déjàvu.

19/

Noriyuki Otsuka Design Office Inc.

Noriyuki Otsuka

Broadly speaking, commercial interior design can be divided into two categories: designs for restaurants and bars, and those for retail establishments. The majority of designers working for the retail industry deal with interiors for boutiques. Noriyuki Otsuka is one of these. Naturally, his work is not restricted to boutique design. He also undertakes commissions for residential projects, cafés, bars, and environment design. As a student, he was fascinated by fashion, and says his field of interest gradually expanded to encompass interiors. Apparel is often said to be architecture in miniature and many similarities can be identified between the two disciplines, such as an emphasis on materials, composition, and design. Considered in this way, fashion design and interior design can be recognized as distant cousins.

Many of Otsuka's works seem at first glance to be almost too simple. The reality, however, is that they contain a host of incredibly delicate features and are rich in subtle nuances that are impossible to grasp merely by looking at photographs. The designer is so enamored of architecture that, during the overseas trips he makes several times a year, he always makes time to tour around various innovative structures, allowing them to influence his ideas. He aims to design "spaces that exist without existing, which seem an amalgam, yet are transparent." The meaning of this abstract utterance can be most easily understood by looking at one of his more recent works, axia "X-rated" in Omotesando Hills.

LE CIEL BLEU Sapporo

Boutique / Sapporo City, Hokkaido / 2005

Stunning LURE Shinsaibashi

Boutique /Chuo-ku, Osaka / 2004

axia "X-rated" Omotesando

Boutique / Shibuya-ku, Tokyo / 2006

Pleats Box

Portable tearoom / 2003

Story

After three years working for a design company, Noriyuki Otsuka decided to quit his job and take a year off. He spent some of it travelling in Europe, a decision that would transform his lifestyle and career. The first city he arrived in was Rome. The following day he took a train to Milan and continued his tour with visits to many Italian towns and cities. Renowned for design, Italy was a place he'd always felt attracted to and he was inspired by countless aspects of the country, from its arid landscape to the shapes of the trees and mountains, from its buildings down to a single pebble lying by the side of the road. He also journeyed into France and Spain. "Looking back, I was in search of my own identity on that trip," he says.

On his return in 1990, he founded his own company at the age of 30. The bubble economy had just started to collapse and it was a time of great financial hardship. "When you set up independently, you become a manager, but you are also working as a designer. I resolved that when I had to settle on a plan of action I would make decisions as a designer, not a manager." Out of this came the determination to only work on projects he was truly interested in.

Otsuka recounts how, in his career to date, his approach has undergone several transformations. "For the first three or four years after becoming independent, I tried for designs that were focused and not particularly playful, expressing a sense of security and using conventional lighting. After that, I went for gallery-like spaces illuminated with white light. I used reds, yellows, and blues to make individual objects stand out from each other clearly, and employed light to heighten the colorful appeal of things I wanted people to focus on. For the last two or

three years, I've become more pre-occupied with light effects, and find myself going in the direction of what's known as contemporary baroque."

The majority of Otsuka's work involves interiors for boutiques. Since the focus in retail is on displaying the products, a recent approach of his has been to dim the global lighting and keep the design from being expressed too strongly in the facade, instead allowing it to make its presence felt throughout the rest of the space. Otsuka blends conventional lighting with more ambient light, as well as that which you'd expect to see in an art gallery; axia "X-rated" in the new Omotesando Hills development is a case in point.

"The truth is I'd like to present people with my designs, but that would risk them being assimilated into prevailing trends. I want to bring out the uniqueness of the designs I create." He warns that the world is increasingly seduced by the glossiness of the images they see. "With any information, what you see still changes depending on the camera angle. There's no way to avoid that, but there are always things that aren't visible in the image. Interior design is just one aspect of the architectural space, and you can't convey everything about the feeling of that space over the net. You can't get across the fact that, though the ceiling is low and the space is narrow, it still feels cozy when you step inside, for example. Or large spaces that still have that slight feeling of tension. The sensations you experience when you walk through the space, the feel of the light, these spatial factors cannot be ignored," he stresses.

Otsuka has a brother, Takahiro, who is 11 years older than him. Based both in Tokyo and their hometown, Takefu City, in Fukui Prefecture, Takahiro works on a diverse range of interiors, from commercial complexes to residential projects such as the Paris home of fashion designer Kenzo Takada. Very few siblings have both managed to make a name for themselves in the world of interior design, and Noriyuki has been greatly influenced by his older brother. When he was at high school, Noriyuki was strongly attracted to fashion design while retaining an interest in radical designs by Milan design collective Memphis, Sottsass and Superstudio.

"The 21st-century architects that I think are truly amazing are people like Jean Nouvel, Rem Koolhaas and Frank Gehry. I think these 21st-century structures have been made possible by the computer age, but you can see them grappling with the challenge of how to present 3-D volumes of architecture in two dimensions. With this in mind, I thought it could be interesting to do interior design, and I'm still trying my hand at it now."

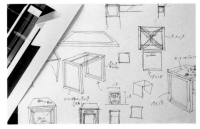

20/

Shuhei Endo Architect Institute

Shuhei Endo

Springtecture, Rooftecture, Bubble-tecture; Shuhei Endo adds the suffix "tecture" to the names of his works to express the form and concept behind each space. The word architecture derives from the Greek *arkhitekton*, meaning a craftsman or builder who has mastered (*arkhi*) the techniques (*tekton*) of manipulating the state and fundamental principles of materials. Similarly, Endo deliberates which techniques fit best with the concept of each of his own projects.

"The first one I came up with was Rooftecture," he explains. "For humans, the most fundamental skill they need when building a structure is that of erecting a roof. I'm not just talking about sacred places, temples, or castles, but the roof that provides shelter over normal houses and workshops." Following on from this, Endo began to alter the first half of the term he'd created to describe his structures according to their shape.

In line with the "paramodern" approach that he advocates, Endo chose to avoid concrete when he was starting out because of its cold, hard weight. Instead, he went for corrugated sheet steel, a material that is both easy to assemble and take apart, and can easily be melted down and used again. Today, although this philosophy remains firmly entrenched in his thinking, he also erects structures out of wood, steel frames and pre-cast concrete.

Bubbletecture M

Kindergarten / Maibara City, Shiga Prefecture / 2003

Bubbletecture O

Private residence / Sakai City, Fukui Prefecture / 2004

Slowtecture Harada

Multipurpose assembly hall / Kamigori, Hyogo Prefecture / 2004

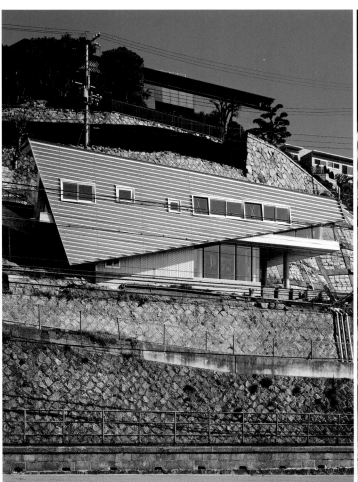

Rooftecture S

Private residence / Kobe City, Hyogo Prefecture / 2005

RODENSTOCK BRILLE GINZA

Glasses store / Chuo-ku, Tokyo / 2005

Halftecture OR

Restaurant and public washrooms / Chuo-ku, Osaka / 2006

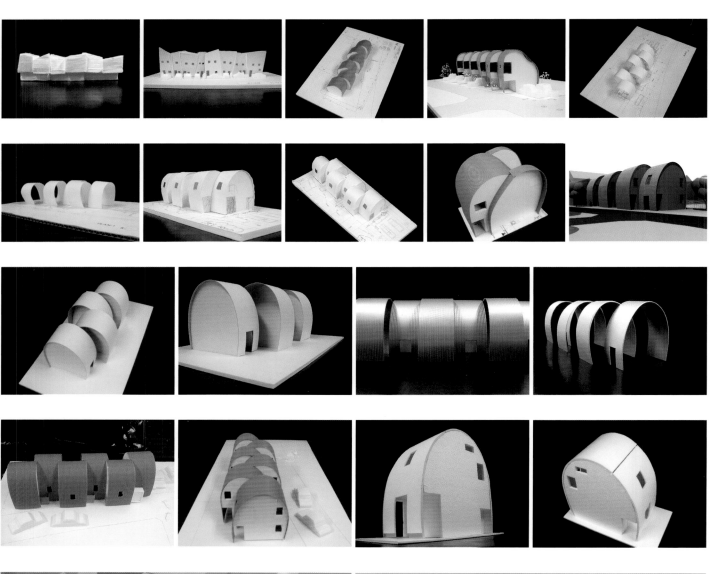

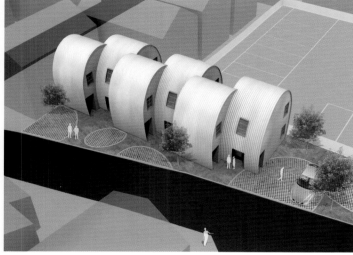

Final rendering

Rooftecture Moris'
(Housing complex /Habikino City, Osaka / Completion expected 2007)

Story

When Shuhei Endo was a sophomore, the classes of Shin Takamatsu, who then lectured part-time at the college, made a huge impression on him. "He had a powerful message and was building structures that didn't seem to obey the rules of architecture," says Endo, readily admitting that Takamatsu's strong personality and style made quite an impact on him. While still a student, Endo took a two-month trip around Europe, visiting 10 countries along the way. Moved by the historic buildings he saw during his trip, he began to wonder why Japanese designers were putting so much energy into following these Western styles of architecture through to their logical conclusion. During his meditations on the subject, an image came to him of the paramodern, a concept he still follows today. On his return home, he was drawn to the writings of philosopher Takeshi Umehara. After a study of Western philosophy, Umehara had moved on to conduct research into the history of Japanese culture, before formulating his own distinctive field of Japanese studies. Endo decided enter the Environmental Design course in the Graduate School of Kyoto City University of Arts, where Umehara was then president.

"I wasn't satisfied with the things I'd learned about architecture at the department of engineering but, at grad school, I had the chance to listen to Umehara's lectures and even have one-to-one conversations with him. Shin Takamatsu was my way into the subject, but Umehara was the person who taught me a standpoint from which to reconsider Japan." As a graduate student, Endo's desire to become an architect was also crystallized through the influence of his advisor. This was Hisayuki Inada, graduate of the architecture course at Tokyo University of Fine Arts and Music.

After completing his studies, Endo entered the offices of Osamu Ishii, founding his own design firm three years later. At that time, one of his clients was major ceramics and tile manufacturer Shino Toseki, which had been built up in the space of one generation by Masahiko Shibatsuji, now turned art critic. Shibatsuji commissioned Endo to produce the design for his new workshop and continued inviting him to work on projects over the following years. The first workshop was a massive undertaking, with a budget of around $2.5million. Since Shino Toseki counted several famous architects among its clients, Shibatsuki was extremely knowledgeable about the field. "He taught me so much of the practical knowledge you need to work as an architect, down to setting up an office and the importance of photographs and records; that was my real initiation into the profession." In 1991, Endo's design for Shino Toseki's third workshop won Italy's Andrea Palladio prize for young architects.

Shuhei Endo uses the word "paramodern" to describe his work. The terms "modern" and "modernism" first came into circulation around 100 years ago and have been in common usage in Japan for many years. Endo believes, however, that their original meaning was lost when the concept was imported to the East. "At its roots, the modernist movement contained the potential for a re-appreciation of abstraction. Paramodernism proposes to explore other possible directions for the modernism now deeply rooted in Japan, taking these inherent possibilities as its starting point."

Over the last 10 years or so, a minimalist trend has been apparent in architecture, but today's minimalism is only skin deep, making no attempt to go beyond the column and beam structures of old. Endo believes that the theory to offer any kind of potential in recent years is paramodern architecture. The corrugated steel he chose as his ideal material is highly democratic: as a manufactured product it is incredibly cheap; and it is also easy to use, meaning that almost anyone can run off a structure. Concrete, on the other hand, takes considerable effort to demolish or move once it has been cast. Corrugated steel requires no welding, but can be held together using small bolts, making it easy to both assemble and take apart. "Corrugated steel eliminates the hierarchy that has existed in architecture until now. Both structurally, and in terms of carrying out a build, established relationships cease to be, and it is here that we are discovering a relative abstraction different from conventional abstraction."

In recent years, Endo has been developing new structures using wood, steel frames and polycarbonate sheets; gradually erasing his image as the corrugated steel architect. For the last decade, he has retained his interest in the architecture of possibility. One of the defining points of architecture is the inability of structures to move, and Endo has persistently found himself speculating what might happen if this weren't the case.

21/

Atelier TEKUTO

Yasuhiro Yamashita

The genesis of any structure begins with both an analysis of the client's demands and the conditions of the site. In their response to these, Yasuhiro Yamashita's houses demonstrate a methodology encompassing both structure and method of construction, expressed through layers, skins, masonry, and panels. For every project, he uncovers the most appropriate structure, construction method, and materials in a process that has resulted in highly unique creations.

Cell Brick, for example, is a massive cube constructed from steel boxes stacked up like bricks. Lucky Drops, on the other hand, is hard to imagine as a house at first glance, such is its design. While ref-ring, which looks like two wooden rings slotted together, offers up new perspectives from each angle of view.

"Since I often work with laypeople, I prefer to avoid abstract descriptions and use more concrete terms instead. And my structures also reflect this tendency," says Yamashita. The designer also has a pragmatic approach based on specifics; an attitude that extends to discussions of cost. "Architects don't usually seem to want to talk about cost. The budget has no relation to the artistic aspects of the work so they tend to dodge the subject. But I always talk about fees, setting things out using concrete figures."

Lucky Drops

Private residence / Setagaya-ku, Toyko / 2005

ref-ring

Private residence / Zushi City,
Kanagawa Prefecture / 2005

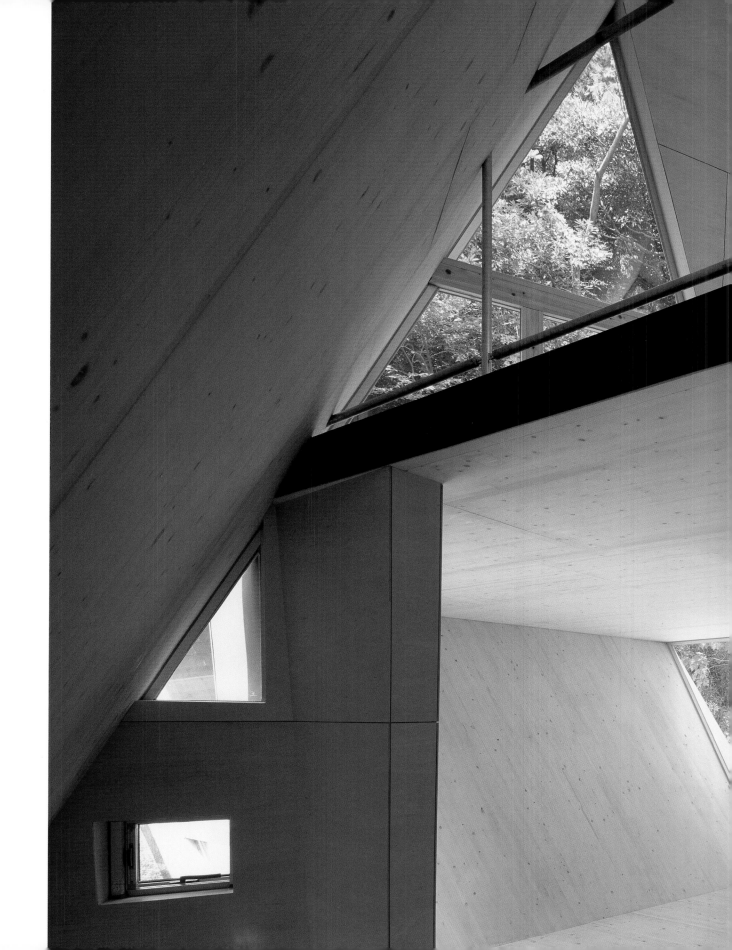

Cell Brick

Private residence / Suginami-ku, Tokyo / 2004

Layers

Private residence / Setagaya-ku, Tokyo / 2005

Story

The houses of Yasuhiro Yamashita offer a wealth of variety, perhaps because he collaborates with a wide variety of other construction professionals. Meeting structural designer Masahiro Ikeda eight years ago produced a turning point in his work. The first project they collaborated on was Y House, completed in 2000. Nicknamed Iron Mask, due the exterior's curious resemblance to a knight's helmet, the project had to take both cost and the north-facing plot into account. The solution was to create a curved wall that would stand up to the strong winds, as well as increase the angle of pitch to further reinforce the structure. According to Yamashita, this piece represents the starting point of the approach he now uses: working together with a structural designer to find solutions to questions of structure, construction methods, and spatiality.

"It's got to the point where we analyze the structure, construction methods, functionality, and thermal environment all together."

When Yamashita first started to discuss the project with Ikeda, the latter man, as a structural designer, had his own ideas about architecture. "Because of that, I can't really say who created the house," admits Yamashita. "There are definitely aspects that we came up with together."

In fact, Yamashita says this is how he can produce such intriguing work. "There are times when I think about structures and building methods that have never been seen before. When I feel the need for something which has no precedent, I take care to carry out all the necessary experiments because I want to come up with something new no matter what."

To achieve this, Yamashita says he consults with designers, structural designers, building contractors, manufacturers, and also universities. Having gathered together the right people, he then tackles the challenge of developing new structures and methods of construction.

The first time Yamashita worked closely with a university was when he had the idea of erecting a three-story wooden structure without the use of structural metal. He was able to call on a man who knew all about timber construction systems, Mikio Koshihara at the University of Tokyo, who was investigating the possibilities offered by timber construction. The results of their collaboration led to Kaminakazato F House, a one-of-a-kind rigid-frame structure entirely supported by n-shaped units.

For another work, Crystal Brick, Yamashita received the support of the largest glass block manufacturer in the industry, Nippon Electric Glass Co. Ltd. For this project, glass bricks were slotted into the holes in the lattice of the steel frame. In his quest to prove that this would work structurally, the designer managed to persuade his project partners to carry out experiment after experiment. Currently, he is collaborating with the Kanazawa Institute of Technology, local government, and various manufacturers to develop houses using aluminum. Other endeavors include designs for exterior foundation insulation using heat- and fire-resistant composite board made out of high-pressure, reinforced cemented excelsior board containing 70 percent natural materials.

Yamashita's heritage blends mainland Japanese and Amami-Oshima island culture. Born on Amami-Oshima, a semi-tropical island occupied by US forces for eight years following the end of World War II, the designer's creations and way of working are open and clear-cut in a way that seems to express a natural openness and warmth inherited from his birthplace. At college, he chose to attend Miyake Riichi's seminars, which opened his eyes to architecture's place in the bigger picture. Under Yutaka Saito in his senior year, he underwent rigorous skills training typified by focused technical drawing practice consisting of marking out 10 parallel lines exactly 1cm apart, over and over again. The point at which he really began to understand architecture was during his time working in the offices of Shunji Kondo, where he learned how planes should be erected and how to bring light into a structure.

Yamashita founded his own firm at the age of 31, but it wasn't entirely smooth sailing at the start. During his first project, Matsushima Watchtower, he learned the knack of working alongside artisans. He found himself sketching out full-sized drawings on site and acting things out to get his ideas across.

In 1995 he renamed his firm Atelier TEKUTO and since then his innovative work has drawn the attention of the world with its succession of unique houses.

The designer's projects are gradually increasing in scale, with 2004 seeing him win an international competition for Busan city's Eco-Center, a work that should be completed in spring 2007.

Ads, Media, Fashion, and Architecture:
Deciphering the Japanese Architectural Design of Today:

Since the 1980s, increasing numbers of Japanese architects and interior designers have been appearing in mass media such as billboards and commercials. Though numbers declined after the economic bubble burst, this trend is now making a comeback following the so-called design boom that occurred around 2004. Rather than remaining mere actors, however, celebrities like Tadao Ando and Toyo Ito are now being seen as cult heroes. Architects are taking on the character of cultural icons; proving to be as interesting when they appear in the media in their everyday clothes as when they are being photographed in funky outfits coordinated by stylists. This new generation of architects is gradually ridding itself of the stereotyped image of the profession. Their work now crosses over genres to embrace structures, products, furniture, graphics, and even performance.

In a male-dominated industry, the activities of female architects are starting to garner more attention. This phenomenon goes hand in hand with a tendency towards employing strategies borrowed from the world of advertising, as well as an escalating degree of collaboration in graphic, product, and web design for commercial architectural and interior projects. Advertising industry publications also feature design and architecture, while there are numerous cases of art directors becoming involved in architectural planning. The way that architects and designers tackle projects via the conceptualizations of an ad-maker is a feature of our times. In Japan today, ties between design, architecture, and advertising are stronger than ever before. Marshall McLuhan's remark that advertising was the greatest art form of the 20th century may be truer than ever in the 21st, though it should be revised to include space design.

By the nature of the profession, many similarities exist between the work of ad-makers, architects, and designers. Each job usually begins with a competition; a concept is devised up for the project; prototypes, models, or samples are presented to the client and, if the bid is successful, they are commissioned to carry the project out. Since authorship is a shared concern of ad-makers and architects, they must prioritize the extent to which they can express their own style at the same time as complying with the client's conditions.

The clearest example of a case blending design, architecture, and advertising lies with Nissan and its commercial strategy. The car manufacturer, realizing that the younger generation was dissatisfied with the interiors of conventional cars whose focus was on hardware, came up with a new advertising strategy highlighting "modern living." Refining its car interiors, it pushed forward with an advertising strategy closely allied to living environment and fashion. In Nissan's TV commercials, their cars elegantly purr past buildings designed by Ken Shuttleworth, speed through those of Santiago Calatrava, or are posed motionless in front of them. The drivers and their partners are fitted out from head to toe in cutting-edge, luxury fashion coor-dinated by experts. Nissan's website not only lists apparel and labels worn by the people in their commercials, but also details such as the name of the famous designer who created the original furniture etc. The message they offer is that a beautiful car is a vital element in a lifestyle enveloped by superb design. An example of a similar design strategy in product advertising is provided by Sharp's plasma TV, Aquos. Thus, while it is becoming harder to distinguish between art and architecture, you could also choose to say that we are seeking to redefine architecture.

Harajuku's Omotesando Hills project, which saw the traditional Dojunkai apartments transformed into a shopping mall, features animated adverts projected onto its exterior. Inside, the space is divided up into hordes of tiny premises occupied by a diverse range of stores. Although the fame of the shopping complex and popularity of its location no doubt raise the cost of leases to an exorbitant level, the mall has been built for tenants who recognize that these boutiques represent not outlets in which to sell products but three dimensional publicity opportunities for the brand. Omotesando Hills is thus less a piece of public art than an immense advertising structure devoted to public relations.

While the leniency of urban building regulations in Japan undeniably holds partial responsibility for the way in which Japanese cities have developed, there is no doubting the high quantity and quality of their architectural and interior designs. People may be unconscious of and thus defenseless against advertising techniques used in space design, but architectural design also greatly increases the value of property. To prevent their works from going to waste in this consumerist climate, architects and interior designers now feel the need to furnish their designs with a power over and above the incitement to consume. In a way, they are incorporating artistic elements and social significance to produce serious works with a signature appeal.

The world of professional architecture, like that of medicine, is closed to lay people and tends to form a kind of sanctuary for its inhabitants. The majority of architects deal directly with clients via their own private firms, or ateliers, and take pride in being members of an elite. On the other side, the public often has no idea of what the actual definition of an architect is, or why those designers working for engineering firms and contractors do not call themselves architects. The situation isn't helped by the traditional images of architecture that are represented by sophisticated magazines and other specialist forms of media. By letting themselves become archives or catalogues of work, magazines have created a rarefied domain incapable of real criticism.

The collapse of the bubble economy saw a marked decrease in the number of commissions for public works from national and local government, and with this source of work disappearing, designers were forced to branch out into other fields. Non-specialist publications such as glossy magazine *Casa BRUTUS* also started presenting architectural design in an attractive, easily comprehensible way that was lapped up by a growing section of the public interested in architecture and interiors.

People in and around the industry as well as architecture-loving members of the public can be defined as the audience for architecture. But the audience for all kinds of design is growing and, while architects and designers certainly don't create works purely for their devotees, and it remains difficult to ascertain the degree of clout that the audience exerts, the new styles of design, and designers, are evidently attracting potential clients. The next generation is likely to attract an ever-stronger audience, which may well extend beyond architecture to encompass those who appreciate all types of contemporary art and culture.

An audience both looks and listens. In classical music, for example, as the awareness of musical influence increases, the professional musician or composer's role of studying classic works in order to reinterpret them for the listener is becoming less important. This same evolution can also be seen in the field of architecture.

In the past, works created by architects had an aura of authority. They were seen as high-quality structures integrating art with technology. Indeed, they outranked interiors, whose design was viewed as a separate and inferior field. Now, however, a new younger generation of designers is emerging; one that is no longer held captive by tradition. Buildings and interiors fused with advertising and fashion multiply, and works are being generated that are free from the shackles of the educational and interpretive impulse. Though this creates the problem of a weakened bond between architectural design and society, audiences today prefer not to seek speculative narratives and instead welcome the secularization of architecture. Many of them profess little interest in authorship yet deify certain masters of the architectural genre as fervently they distinguish between fashion labels. It is impossible to ignore the influence that images of architects and their works generated by the media have on the design literacy of the audience. The new audience takes no account of history in its appreciation of a work. Over and above context or background information, they tend to place a matter-of-fact emphasis on what lies before them: the colors and forms, materials, functions, structure, and novelty of the ideas expressed.

As more and more Western-style architecture is transplanted to Japan, contemporary architectural design appears to be quietly slipping out of the solid framework of tradition. It is therefore possible that the lightness and focus on refinement of skills at the heart of Japanese culture will be brought to bear on realizing structures with a high potential for flexibility.

When visualizing the new generation of architectural design, the most important keyword after "advertising" has to be "fashion". If clothes are said to be our second skin, buildings must surely be the third. The smallest structure has to address all the basic requirements of fashion: construction, function, materials, design, air conductivity, durability, social significance, weather, and safety of the user. Architecture of every era has been influenced not only by artistic concerns but, like apparel, by the lifestyles, fashions, and values of its time. Taking the metaphor of structures as apparel a little further, contemporary architecture, typified by CAD and structural risk taking, prioritizes a number of concerns that can be directly translated to fashion design: namely, lightness, colorful style, transparency, plasticity, audacious forms, development of new materials, insistence on natural materials (and fusion of these), the revival of physical sensation, artistic orientation, and integration with the media. In this light, these must also be recognized as the elements sought by the spirit of the age.

Recent examples of the increasingly close relationship between architecture and fashion can be found in Kosuke Tsumura's fashion design that treats clothing as the smallest shelter, and in Hussein Chalayan's work, which is informed by architectural and spatial design concepts. Not long ago, Tiffany Japan commissioned Frank Gehry to design a jewelry collection; such architects active in the fields of furniture and product design have been around for decades. Architecture is both tactile and visual, and the words of Walter Benjamin in *The Work of Art in the Age of Mechanical Reproduction* retain their relevance.

Richard Bolton's 1988 essay on Hennessy advertising[1].-which debated the weakening of the architect's image-appeared at a time when architects were being criticized and losing the authority and social significance they once laid claim to. To trace an interesting coincidence, in 1987 the Hennessy Corporation merged with Louis Vuitton to become the conglomerate LVMH, whose joint concern LVP created fashion label Prada. Later, Prada commissioned Pritzker prizewinners Herzog and de Meuron to design their Aoyama flagship store. The result is a structure shaped like a gigantic bottle of perfume that manages to give physical form to the atmosphere enveloping both the age and its products. In this way, architectural design certainly seems destined to approach ever closer the expression of a third skin.

1. Richard Bolton "Architecture and cognac" in John Thackara, *Design After Modernism* (Thames and Hudson, 1988)

01/
MOUNT FUJI
ARCHITECTS
STUDIO
Masahiro Harada + MAO

P9
XXXX-House

Principal use: Ceramics studio
Location: Yaizu City,
Shizuoka Prefecture
Completion date: 2003
Site area: 502.86 square meters
Building area: 22.3 square meters
Total floor area: 16.7 square meters
Type of structure: Wood panel
construction, one floor above ground
Description: A small, timber monocoque
structure used as a ceramics studio:
constructed out of four to five panelized
1800-by-900-by-12 millimeter sheets of
standard structural plywood. This DIY
structure took three days to erect. The
lack of columns produces excellent
lighting and ventilation. The X-shaped
frame of units gives the possibility of
expansion; plans exist to extend it in the
future.

P11
Light-Light Shelter

Principal use: Delicatessen
Location: Yaizu City,
Shizuoka Prefecture
Completion date: 2004
Site area: 122.31 square meters
Building area: 97.1 square meters
Total floor area: 86.13 square meters
Type of structure: Steel construction,
one floor above ground
Structural design: Jun Sato Structural
Architects
Description: A delicatessen featuring
an N-shaped frame constructed out of
four hyperbolic paraboloid shell units.
Slits allowing in light and trusses are
found at the joins between units,
resulting in a strong, yet light, tube-
shaped structure that maximizes the
floor area, while minimizing volume of
steel frame. Natural light entering
through the slits is softened by the
hyperbolic paraboloids in the roof to
diffuse through the entire interior.

P12
Secondary Landscape

Principal use: Roof garden and salon
Location: Shibuya-ku, Tokyo
Completion date: 2004
Total floor area: 75.72 square meters
Type of structure: Steel construction
(existing structure: reinforced concrete
construction)
Structural design: Jun Sato Structural
Architects
Description: A remodeling of the roof
and roof storage of a beauty school
housed in a 40-year-old reinforced
concrete structure. The roof was
covered in red cedar angled into
polygonal planes to add variety and
make it seem like a changing landscape,
transforming the roof into a gathering
place for the young creators. Convertible
cabinets and steel tables are original
works.

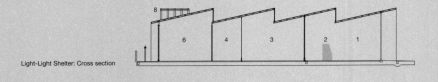

Light-Light Shelter: Cross section

1: Sales floor
2: Counter
3: Side dish kitchen
4: Processed meats kitchen
5: Toilet
6: Office
7: Refrigerator
8: Cooling unit

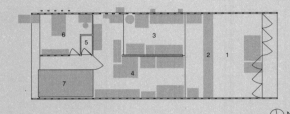

Light-Light Shelter: Floor plan

1/250　N

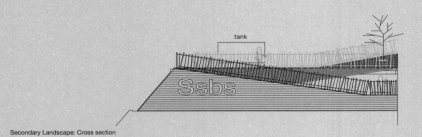

Secondary Landscape: Cross section

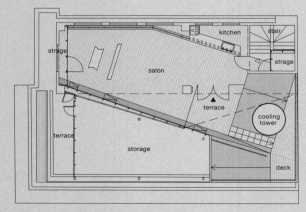

Secondary Landscape: Rooftop-floor plan

Secondary Landscape: Sixth-floor plan

1/250　N

02/
TORAFU
ARCHITECTS
Koichi Suzuno +
Shinya Kamuro

P17
TEMPLATE IN CLASKA

Principal use: Hotel guest room
Location: Meguro-ku, Tokyo
Completion date: 2004
Total floor area: 18 square meters by
three rooms
Description: A remodeling of the long-
term guest rooms in Hotel CLASKA in
Meguro, Tokyo. The idea of inserting
hotel room and travel items into
openings in the wall grew out of the
difficult conditions created by the tight
space and low budget. The result is a
unique work that brought TORAFU to
international attention.

P20
SPINNING OBJECTS

Principal use: Showroom
Location: Fuchu City, Tokyo
Completion date: 2004
Total floor area: 167 square meters
Joint furniture design: Taiji Fujimori
Atelier
Description: As a showroom for a
trading company specializing in hotel
toiletries, this space had to give equal
space and attention to an overwhelming
number of different sizes, types, colors,
and shapes of product. The design
store's products pack away neatly, and
the space dares to play with a
proliferation of images without feeling
chaotic.

P22
TABLE ON THE ROOF

Principal use: A multi-purpose space
on a hotel rooftop
Location: Meguro-ku, Tokyo
Completion date: 2004
Total floor area: 240 square meters
Description: Adding a 55-centimeter-
high deck to the roof of Hotel CLASKA
created a surface that people can
stand or sit upon. It can also be used
as a stage, or viewed as an enormous
table, with chairs positioned around the
edge. The interest lies in its ambiguity
of purpose.

P23
ReBITA

Principal use: Office
Location: Shibuya-ku, Tokyo
Completion date: 2005
Total floor area: 176 square meters
Description: One side of the partition
walls in this office renovation can be
used as display boards for building
material samples, while the other
features storage boxes for books, and
so on. Since the storage is set at an
angle, the contents are never completely
visible. The structure can be easily taken
apart, adding to its convenience.

P24
UDS SHANGHAI OFFICE

Principal use: Office
Location: Shanghai, China
Completion date: 2005
Total floor area: 86 square meters
Description: An office featuring glass
partitions masked with mirrored strips
which assimilate the reflection into the
view beyond. Curious, subtle effects
are generated by stripes of reflected
light; the interior carries off the optical
illusion of making the small, triangular
room appear much larger.

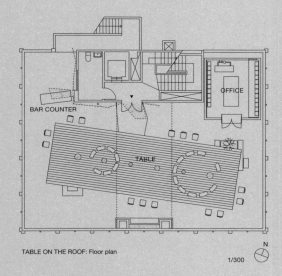

TABLE ON THE ROOF: Floor plan   1/300

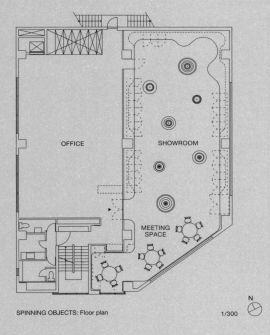

SPINNING OBJECTS: Floor plan   1/300

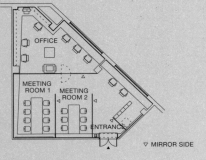

UDS SHANGHAI OFFICE: Floor plan   1/300

03/
NAP Architects
Hiroshi Nakamura

P27
LANVIN BOUTIQUE GINZA

Principal use: Boutique
Location: Ginza, Chuo-ku, Tokyo
Completion date: 2004
Total floor area: 874.99 square meters
Type of structure: Steel construction,
part RC, three floors
Description: An interior and exterior
remodeling that introduces a house-
like façade into the wall of the existing
building. Using a special technique,
roughly 3000 acrylic cylinders have
been inserted into the steel plate of the
façade. The décor and furniture design
are also included in the project.

P29
House SH

Principal use: Private residence
Location: Minato-ku, Tokyo
Completion date: 2005
Site area: 40.85 square meters
Building area: 24.5 square meters
Total floor area: 86.97 square meters
Type of structure: RC construction,
three floors: one floor below ground
Structural design: SHU TADA
STRUCTURAL CONSULTANTS
Description: Skylights bring sunlight
through the lightwell down into this
structure, which is built to take
maximum advantage of a vertical use
of space while maximizing coverage
ratio by extending walls to the outer
edges of the plot. The wall recess
allows tactile communication with the
structure, proposing an intimate
relationship between the structure and
its inhabitants.

P30
Lotus Beauty Salon

Principal use: Beauty salon
Location: Kuwana City, Mie Prefecture
Completion date: 2006
Site area: 763.59 square meters
Building area: 330.72 square meters
Total floor area: 626.43 square meters
Type of structure: Steel construction,
part RC
Structural design: Structural Design
Office OAK
Description: Circular booths are scattered throughout a space that remains
openplan above a certain height to get
the best of both worlds. The floor
slopes in line with the natural cant of
the plot, so the breast wall takes on
different functions as you move further
inside, from bench to desk to counter
to partition, creating an interior
boasting private rooms without feeling
claustrophobic.

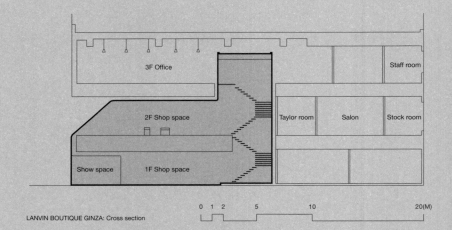

LANVIN BOUTIQUE GINZA: Cross section

0 1 2   5   10   20(M)

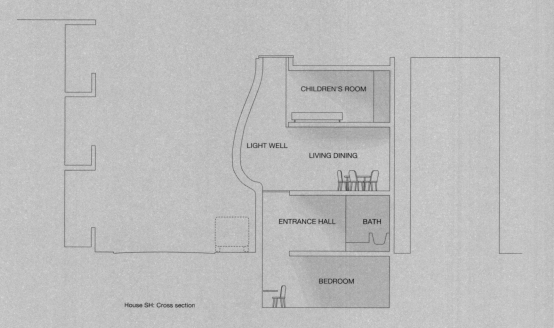

House SH: Cross section

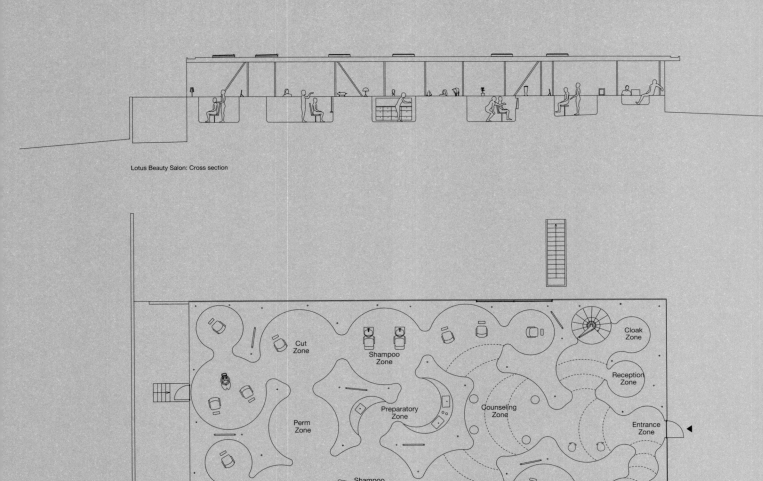

Lotus Beauty Salon: Cross section

Lotus Beauty Salon: Floor plan

1/200

Cut Zone

Shampoo Zone

Perm Zone

Preparatory Zone

Counseling Zone

Cloak Zone

Reception Zone

Entrance Zone

Cut Zone

Shampoo Zone

Cut Zone

Waiting Zone

04/
TONERICO: INC.
Hiroshi Yoneya +
Ken Kimizuka +
Yumi Masuko

P36
ANYA

Principal use: *Wagashi* store and
teahouse
Location: Seijo, Setagaya-ku, Tokyo
Completion date: 2004
Total floor area: 102.9 square meters
Design: Ken Kimizuka
Cooperation: Lighting design/Yuko
Yamashita (Y2 lighting design),
Graphic design/Nanako Kamiya
Description: A place to relax and enjoy
freshly-prepared *wagashi* while gazing
at the spot-lit courtyard garden
through a glass wall flowing with
water. Three moveable central panels
covered in handmade *washi* paper
preserve a sense of privacy and can be
used to partition off a private room.
Wood, stone, glass, paper, water; the
natural beauty of the materials used
harmonizes perfectly with the Japanese
confectionary.

P37
JUS de COEUR

Principal use: Juice bar
Location: Nishi-Shinjuku,
Shinjuku-ku, Tokyo
Completion date: 2005
Total floor area: 15.52 square meters
Design: Hiroshi Yoneya
Planning: Yukio Aihara, Kikuko
Fujimoto (Studio Cultivate)
Cooperation: Graphic design/Osamu
Ohuchi (nano/nano graphics)
Description: A juice bar located inside
Shinjuku station's West Exit serving
exclusively Nepuree juices that keep the
fiber in the pulped fruit and vegetables
intact, allowing customers to enjoy the
flavors of each season. Mirrored surfaces
make the bar seem to melt away into its
bustling surroundings to create a space
that, despite assimilation with its
environment, has a powerful presence.

P38
KIKYOYA

Principal use: *Wagashi* store and
teahouse
Location: Mizuho, Nagoya City,
Aichi Prefecture
Completion date: 2005
Site area: 399.99 square meters
Building area: 130.08 square meters
Total floor area: 222.2 square meters
Type of structure: Steel construction,
two floors above ground
Design: Hiroshi Yoneya, Ken Kimizuka
Cooperation: Lighting design/Yuko
Yamashita (Y2 lighting design),
Logo design/Shirohide Azuma (WHITE
Phat Graphics)
Description: Almost every surface in
this interior features pale stucco, based
on the delicate subtlety of the store's
famous *Nobori Yokan*. In an effective
visual device, pushing aside the *noren*
curtains at the entrance reveals the
store's symbol, a sculptural metal
object; water welling forth expresses
one of the vital ingredients of *wagashi*
confectionary. A tabletop laser cut with
the family crest is calculated to cast
beautiful shadows on the floor.

P40
MEMENTO @ le bain

Principal use: Installation
Location: Nishi-Azabu,
Minato-ku, Tokyo
Completed: 2005
Total floor area: Gallery 61.04 square
meters, patio 50.87 square meters
Design: Hiroshi Yoneya, Yumi Masuko
Cooperation: Lighting design/Yuko
Yamashita (Y2 lighting design)
Description: An installation built of
layers of code in images and memory,
this piece, whose concept is "hidden
world," transcends the normal space,
and is further complicated by use and
ornamentation. Memento is a touring
installation. (Pictures taken at Tokyo's
Gallery le Bain.)

P42
TAMATOSHI + ACRYS

Principal use: Showroom
Location: Iwamoto-cho,
Chiyoda-ku, Tokyo
Completion date: 2005
Total floor area: First floor 85.06
square meters, Second floor 94.87
square meters
Design: Ken Kimizuka
Cooperation: Lighting design/Yuko
Yamashita (Y2 lighting design)
Description: A hanger and acrylic product
showroom, in which colors and materials
on the first floor are muted to make the
neatly suspended products the only
things that stand out, while the second
floor features a faintly luminescent main
wall consisting of layered frosted glass
and colored panels that fuse the
transparent products into the space.

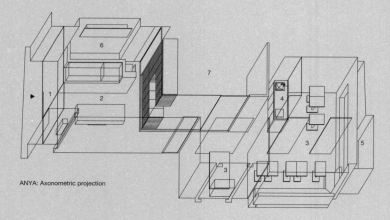

ANYA: Axonometric projection

1: Entrance
2: Shop
3: Tearoom
4: Tearoom pantry
5: Glass/water screen and
   courtyard garden
6: Pantry
7: *Wagashi* preparation room

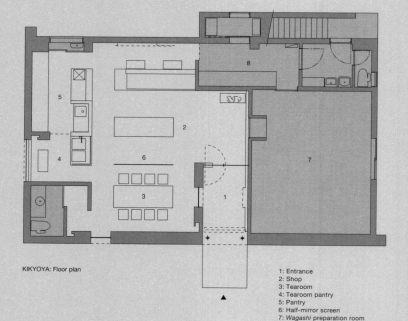

KIKYOYA: Floor plan

1: Entrance
2: Shop
3: Tearoom
4: Tearoom pantry
5: Pantry
6: Half-mirror screen
7: *Wagashi* preparation room
8: Pantry

05/
SKSK architects
Keiichiro Sako

P46
T in Tokyo

Principal use: Handcrafted jewelry shop
Location: Hiroo, Shibuya-ku, Tokyo
Completion date: 2003
Total floor area: 20 square meters
Description: A tiny handcrafted jewelry shop facing a busy road whose 10 square-meter-façade features mirror-finished steel panels decorated in a looping pattern drawn with a grinder. Throughout the day, its appearance metamorphoses with changes in natural light and reflections from nearby stoplights, car lamps, and light from surrounding buildings. Shining spotlights on the worktop inside has made its circular patterns appear to float above the table surface.

P47
FELISSIMO in Beijing

Principal use: Boutique
Location: Beijing, China
Completion date: 2004
Total floor area: 330 square meters
Description: Cubic furniture in two sizes, 400-by-400-by-400 millimeters and 400-by-400-by-800 millimeters, was proposed as the standard units of this interior. Each box-like piece can connect to the other both horizontally and vertically, and can be fitted with mirrors, signs, lighting or metal tubes that act as hanging rails. At night, the neon tube lights on the ceiling are multiplied to infinity in the reflective glass.

P48
Kid's Republic in Beijing

Principal use: Bookstore
Location: Beijing, China
Completion date: 2005
Total floor area: 165.50 square meters (First floor 57.70 square meters, Second floor 107.80 square meters)
Description: A Beijing bookstore housing a first-floor event space and second-floor children's bookstore. Lighting and display shelves are installed into ceiling, walls and floor, whose different levels can be used as stage and audience seating. A 100 meter-long rainbow starts at the entrance and unfurls throughout the interior, ascending the stairs before winding through the bookstore in many guises before returning downstairs as the staircase handrail. Circular openings in the walls act as reading spaces and windows, allowing the store's fun interior to broadcast its appeal to the outside world.

P51
Storage in Tokyo

Principal use: Storage space and offices
Location: Ome, Koto-ku, Tokyo
Completion date: 2005
Total floor area: 3000 square meters
Description: The concept was an animated storage area constructed in a single framework. Color was used to give the various elements (stock shelving, workshop, offices, and breakroom) within the 3,000-square-meter remo-deled space a unified identity

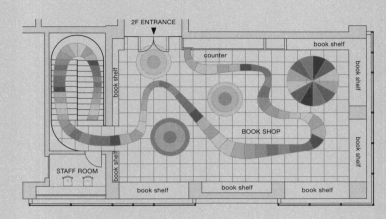

Kid's Republic in Beijing: Second-floor plan

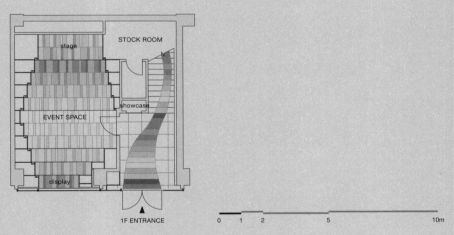

Kid's Republic in Beijing: First-floor plan

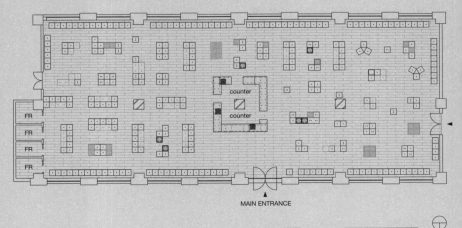

Felissimo in Beijing: Floor plan

06/
TEZUKA
ARCHITECTS
Takaharu + Yui
Tezuka

P56
Echigo-Matsunoyama
Museum of Natural Science
Matsunoyama, Niigata

Principal use: Natural Science Museum
Location: Matsunoyama, Tokamachi City, Niigata Prefecture
Completion date: 2003
Site area: 4,269.15 square meters
Building area: 997.45 square meters
Total floor area: 1,248.18 square meters
Type of structure: Steel construction, one floor below ground, two floors above ground
Design: Takaharu+Yui Tezuka/Tezuka Architects; collaborative design by Masahiro Ikeda/MASAHIRO IKEDA co., ltd.
Description: A natural science-based educational and research facility located in Niigata's Matsunoyama area, where heavy snowfall can exceed 30 meters in winter, this structure is 160 meters in length and boasts a 34 meter-high tower. Windows are made of heavyweight acrylic; the largest sheet measures 14.5 meters across by four meters high, and weighs roughly four tons. Despite its tube-like shape, each section in the building has an open feel. The facility caters to resident natural scientists, as well as being open to the public.

P58
Roof House

Principal use: Private residence
Location: Kanagawa Prefecture
Completion date: 2001
Site area: 298.59 square meters
Building area: 107.65 square meters
Total floor area: 96.89 square meters
Type of structure: Timber construction, one floor
Design: Takaharu+Yui Tezuka/Tezuka Architects; collaborative design by Masahiro Ikeda/MASAHIRO IKEDA co., ltd.
Description: A design that grants the clients' wish to be able to eat outside on their roof, which, at 139 square meters, covers a greater area than the interior of the house. Completely covered in a wood deck, the surface has been equipped with kitchen, chairs and table, around which an L-shaped 1.2-meter-high wall acts as a windbreak and preserves their privacy. Eight skylights mean that each room below has more than one; some also provide access to the roof. Constructed of 105-centimeter-square pieces of structural plywood sandwiched together, the roof is 150 millimeters thick and has a one-tenth pitch.

P59
Engawa House

Principal use: Private residence
Location: Tokyo
Completion date: 2003
Site area: 196.27 square meters
Building area: 74.48 square meters
Total floor area: 74.48 square meters
Type of structure: Timber construction, part steel frame, one floor
Design: Takaharu+Yui Tezuka/Tezuka Architects; collaborative design by Masahiro Ikeda/MASAHIRO IKEDA co., ltd.
Description: To preserve the garden to the north and allow the residents to share it with the main house, the long, narrow structure follows the road planned for the south side. A 2.2-meter-wall was constructed to face the road and sidelights inserted above that, preserving privacy while affording a good view of the sky. The L-shaped structure is 16.2 meters in length and 4.6 meters deep, and boasts a long stretch of nine sliding glass doors to turn the whole house into a veranda.

P60
Observatory House

Principal use: Private residence
Location: Kanagawa Prefecture
Completion date: 2004
Site area: 136.50 square meters
Building area: 54.45 square meters
Total floor area: 175.09 square meters
Type of structure: Steel construction, one floor below ground, three floors above ground
Design: Takaharu+Yui Tezuka/Tezuka Architects; collaborative design by Masahiro Ikeda/MASAHIRO IKEDA co., ltd.
Description: Due to building restrictions, a two-story steel-frame house was erected on a large concrete stage supported by a central core, making the upper floors into an observatory rising above neighboring buildings to overlook the coast. The inner glass doors can be flung open and outer wooden louvers closed so that even on rainy days the fresh sea breezes can enter.

P62
Eaves House

Principal use: Private residence
Location: Saitama Prefecture
Completion date: 2006
Site area: 297.61 square meters
Building area: 119.57 square meters
Total floor area: 119.57 square meters
Type of structure: Steel construction, one floor
Design: Takaharu+Yui Tezuka/Tezuka Architects; collaborative design by Masahiro Ikeda/MASAHIRO IKEDA co., ltd.
Description: Four meters below the west-side retaining wall of this building lies the dry bed of an old brook, and the design follows this line. This project has dispensed with the usual concept of a house to create an open space without supporting columns on two sides, allowing the floor to extend beyond the glass of the sliding doors right to the lot line.

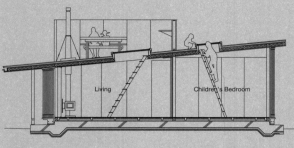

Roof House: Cross section   1/60

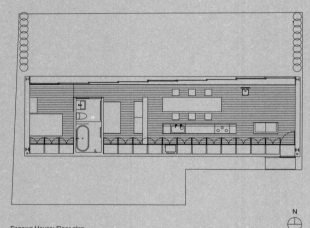

Engawa House: Floor plan

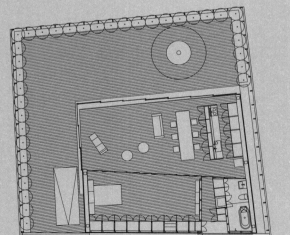

Eaves House: Floor plan

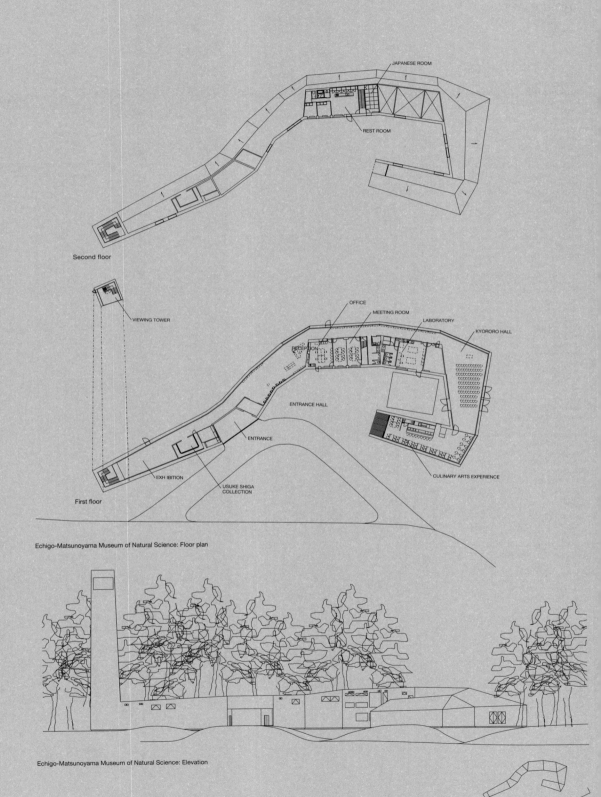

Second floor

JAPANESE ROOM

REST ROOM

VIEWING TOWER

OFFICE

MEETING ROOM

LABORATORY

KYORORO HALL

RECEPTION

ENTRANCE HALL

ENTRANCE

EXHIBITION

USUKE SHIGA COLLECTION

CULINARY ARTS EXPERIENCE

First floor

Echigo-Matsunoyama Museum of Natural Science: Floor plan

Echigo-Matsunoyama Museum of Natural Science: Elevation

07/
GLAMOROUS
Co., Ltd.
Yasumichi Morita

P68
MEGU New York

Principal use: Japanese restaurant
Location: New York, USA
Completion date: 2004
Total floor area: 1,300 square meters
Cooperation: Design/Satomi Hatanaka (GLAMOROUS Co. Ltd.), Seiji Sakagami,
Consultant/Osamu Hashimoto, Sachiko M Masaki (Hashimoto & Partners Inc.),
Photo/Mitsuhiro Susa
Ukiyoe art/Gaku Azuma
Description: Located in Manhattan's Tribeca area, this restaurant employs Seto earthenware, kimono fabric, lacquerware, earthen walls, and bamboo screens to present a non-stereotypical Japanese beauty. The first floor features an enormous Japanese flag and delicate towers of pottery from Seto bolted together to hold them in place. From the ceiling above the atrium space in the main dining area hangs an immense temple bell (made from FRP, weighing 500 kilograms, measuring three meters tall by two meters in diameter). The east wall of this dining room features bamboo screens; the west porcelain tiles.

P70
ZETTON CAFE & EATS

Principal use: Café
Location: Central Japan International Airport, Aichi Prefecture
Completion date: 2005
Total floor area: 147 square meters
Cooperation: Design/Yoshiaki Sumitomo, Lighting (DAIKO ELECTRIC CO., LTD.)
Description: The designer, a tobacco-lover, designed what could be a VIP lounge for smokers in the passenger terminal of Central Japan International Airport, located near Tokoname City in Aichi Prefecture. The café offers a large number of counter seats offering an uninterrupted view of the check-in desks.

P71
TOKIA (Tokyo Building)

Principal use: Public space in a commercial complex
Location: Marunouchi, Chiyoda-ku, Tokyo
Completion date: 2005
Total floor area: Basement 840 square meters, Second floor 240 square meters, Third floor 315 square meters
Cooperation: Design/Daisuke Watanabe, Custom-made tiles/DINAONE Corporation, Lighting/DAIKO ELECTRIC CO., LTD., Custom-made lamps/nets 101 Co., Ltd., WISEWORK, Other/TEN-NEN-SHA INC.
Description: Environment design of public space on the basement, second and third floors of Toyko Building. To lend a sense of connectedness to the shops and combat the tendency towards monotony in the basement mall, vertical and horizontal light boxes were positioned to run through the space, adding variety to it and arousing visitors' curiosity. These boxes fill the role of lighting, signs and even benches. The floor of the second and third floors is laid in a herringbone pattern reminiscent of sidewalks, while wire mesh lamps along the walkways and in the elevators again add variety.

P72
SJX

Principal use: Men's jewelry and accessory shop
Location: Jingu-Mae, Shibuya-ku, Tokyo
Completion date: 2004
Total floor area: 68.12 square meters
Cooperation: Design/Takuma Sato, Lighting/Kenji Ito (MAXRAY inc.)
Description: Men's jewelry and accessory shop located on the second floor of Omotesando Hills. Curtains created from 110,000 octagonal crystals in black and topaz, inspired by opera house stage curtains, lend the space a certain dignity and produce a feeling of anticipation in visitors who have come to see the latest pieces. Jet-black champagne bottles bring out the beauty of the jewelry even further.

P74
MEGU Midtown

Principal use: Japanese restaurant
Location: New York, USA
Completion date: 2004
Total floor area: First floor 264 square meters, Middle floor 105 square meters
Cooperation: Design/Shingo Abe, Aki Sakuramoto (GLAMOROUS Co.,Ltd.), Consulting/Toshi Enterprise INC., Photo/Mitsuhiro Susa
Ukiyoe art/Gaku Azuma
Description: The concept was a mixture of Japanese traditional and modern. Massive lampshades were designed to make the most of the numerous pillars while other elements, including wooden beads carved into family crests, chair backs in Japanese fabric, photographs, and scenic images such as carp and seas of clouds taken from Ukiyoe art, combine to produce a dramatic interior.

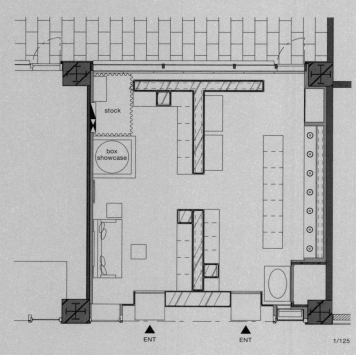

SJX: Floor plan

1/125

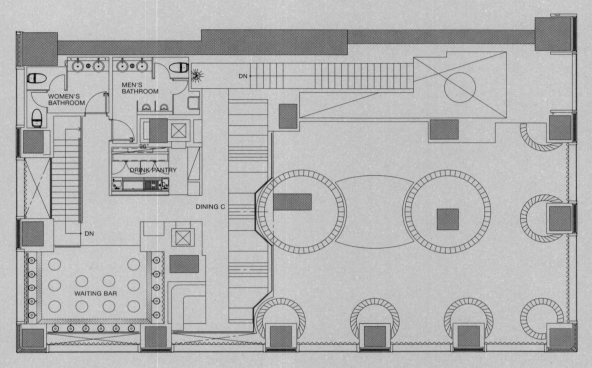

MEGU Midtown: Middle- floor plan

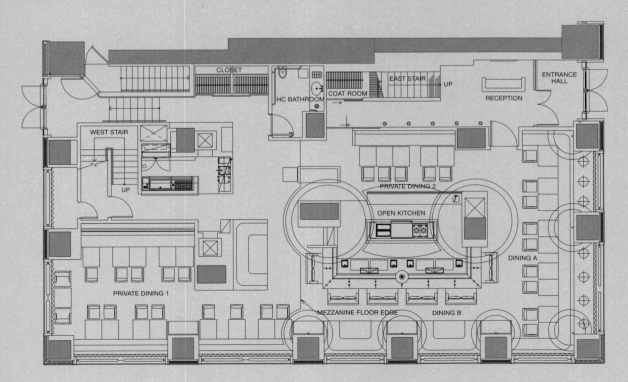

MEGU Midtown: Middle- floor plan

08/
FANTASTIC
DESIGN WORKS
Katsunori Suzuki

P79
J-POP Cafe Odaiba

Principal use: Restaurant
Location: Odaiba, Minato-ku, Tokyo
Completion date: 2002
Total floor area: 625.03 square meters
Description: Situated in Sega's Tokyo Joypolis, this café features an organic, analog design to contrast with the surrounding game center. The majority of fixtures are made of solid, molded plaster. The approach from the outside deck is a long tunnel that leads right into the center of the space.

P81
J-POP Cafe Taipei

Principal use: Restaurant
Location: Chung Hsiao East Road, Taipei, Taiwan
Completion date: 2002
Total floor area: 500 square meters
Description: Located in Bistro 98, Taipei's first tower block devoted entirely to dining, the seventh floor entrance opens onto an approach leading down to the sixth floor main hall. To allow the maximum number of tables to enjoy the images, mirrors reflect them at an angle below the projection screen. The seventh floor features round tables and lounges to cater for groups, while the floor below boasts a stage and long central counter for a club-like feel, giving each space a distinctive character.

P82
Alux

Principal use: Lounge and dining bar
Location: Minami-Aoyama, Minato-ku, Tokyo
Completion date: 2006
Total floor area: 474.49 square meters
Wall relief: Motif design by Kelly Chen
Description: The theme of total luxury unites this bar, lounge, and restaurant. The enormous plaster bas-relief on the main dining hall wall was based on a drawing by Hong Kong actress Kelly Chan while Armani Japan produced the uniforms of the wait staff.

P84
Ikebukuro Otogibanashi

Principal use: Entrance
Location: Minami-Ikebukuro, Toshima-ku, Tokyo
Completion date: 2005
Total floor area: 37.72 square meters
Description: At the bottom of the staircase leading from this curious, sparkling white entrance lie four restaurants, each based on a different magical fantasy. The Wizard of The Opera is themed around the story of the Phantom of the Opera, while Ryugu features a chinoiserie décor based on the Dragon King's palace that lies at bottom of the ocean. There are also two other Japanese restaurants.

Blue Lounge RYUGU

Principal use: Bar
Location: Minami-Ikebukuro, Toshima-ku, Tokyo
Completion date: 2005
Total floor area: 50.416 square meters

GORGEOUS&GOTHIC DINING THE WIZARD OF THE OPERA

Principal use: Dining bar
Location: Minami-Ikebukuro, Toshima-ku, Tokyo
Completion date: 2005
Total floor area: 154.589 square meters

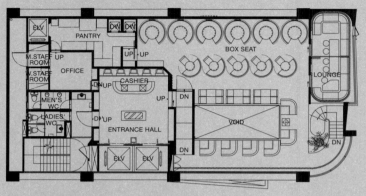

J-POP Cafe Taipei: Seventh-floor plan

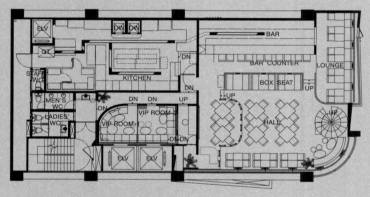

J-POP Cafe Taipei: Sixth-floor plan

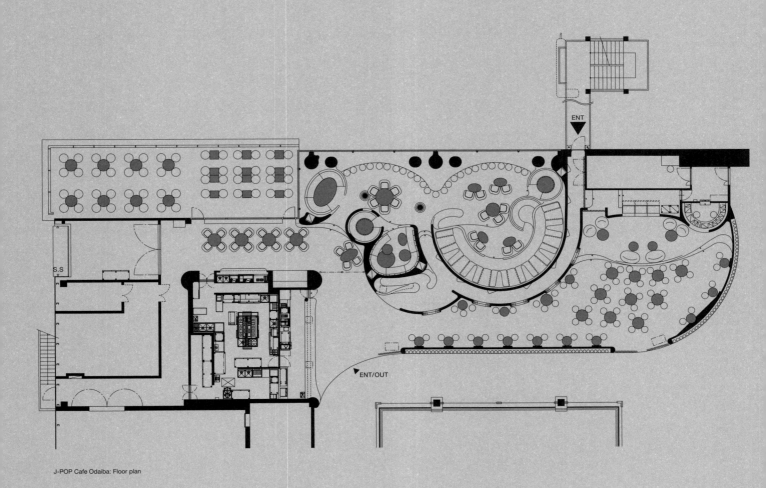

J-POP Cafe Odaiba: Floor plan

09/
cafe co.
Yoshiyuki Morii

P87
K-two Aoyama

Principal use: Beauty salon
Location: Minami-Aoyama,
Minato-ku, Tokyo
Completion date: 2004
Total floor area: 328.7 square meters
Description: Trees have been planted
in the center of the cutting zone of this
salon and enclosed in glass, producing
the surreal impression of looking out
into nature. Natural motifs are
scattered throughout the space—
lighting pours down like sunlight
through leaves; the cold-cut zone
features a waterfall, logs, and rippling
ceiling panels—creating an extremely
relaxing interior.

P89
M residence

Principal use: Private residence
Location: Kobe City, Hyogo Prefecture
Completion date: 2004
Site area: 114.51m square meters
Building area: 68.58 square meters
Total floor area: 146.67 square meters
Type of structure: Steel frame
construction, two floors
Structural design: IMADA Structural
design
Description: For this sloping lot in
Rokko, Kobe, which overlooks Kobe
Bay and adjoins a promenade lined
with cherry trees, the concept was to
bring the lush mountain landscape and
stunning views inside. The plan
consisted of remodeling the existing
two-story wooden structure by taking
advantage of the artificial ground it
was built on and rebuilding the upper
portion in steel. The space underneath
was made into a guest and shower
room.

P90
Bishoku MAIMON Umeda

Principal use: Japanese restaurant
Location: Umeda, Kita-ku, Osaka
Completion date: 2004
Total floor area: 251.27 square meters
Description: "A Stadium of Cuisine"
was the design concept and, to
achieve this look, designers introduced
a circular hood covered in images
featuring the craftsmen and origins of
luxury ingredients from around Japan,
below which the chefs would display
their talents.

P91
Ristorante Versare

Principal use: Wedding hall
Location: Oiwake, Kusatsu City,
Shiga Prefecture
Completion date: 2005
Total floor area: 155.84 square meters
Description: A chapel of light enveloped in 1,350 aluminum pipes and
surrounded on all sides by glass, this
space makes visitors aware of the
changing natural light. At night, floor
lighting brings full expression to the
pipes and transforms the building into a
glowing landmark.

P92
Maison de Comtesse

Principal use: Beauty salon
Location: Shinsaibashi,
Chuo-ku, Osaka
Completion date: 2005
Total floor area: 131.45 square meters
Description: Located in a department
store in Shinsaibashi, Osaka, whose
aim is for people to relive the halcyon
days of the covered shopping street
Shinsaihashi-suji, this salon greets
customers with the façade of a
European-style house. In line with its
name, the designer went for elegant,
organic motifs to create a healing
space with an aura of quality.

P94
danceteria SAZA*E

Principal use: Club
Location: Chayamachi, Kita-ku, Osaka
Completion date: 2005
Total floor area: First floor 158.2
square meters, Middle floor 58.5
square meters, Second floor 264.3
square meters, Second-middle floor
43.8 square meters, Third floor 222.5
square meters, Fourth floor 261 square
meters
Description: Five floors whose various
looks come from the overall concept of
sazae—the sea snail's shell's spiraling
patterns. The second floor dance hall
features a mezzanine housing the VIP
room; above, the artwork display floor
appeals to adults through the classic
sophistication of its wall design, while
the fourth-floor Flamingo consists of a
relaxed poolside-dining zone.

P96
Tab Device Aoyama

Principal use: Boutique
Location: Minami-Aoyama,
Minato-ku, Tokyo
Completion date: 2004
Total floor area: First floor 63.5 square
meters, Second floor 66.2 square
meters
Description: The new Levi's concept
store is themed along a fraternity: the
interior incorporates music and sport
in a bid to make teenage customers
see the brand in a new light. Laid out
like a house, it embodies a youthful
lifestyle. The two horses symbolizing
the brand reappear here in a surreal
setting. The name of the store comes
from "Red Tab device," the old Levi's
practice of affixing a red tab to its
jeans to give them a rough idea of their
market share.

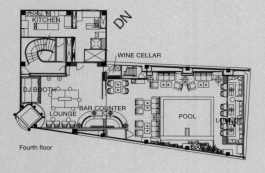

Fourth floor

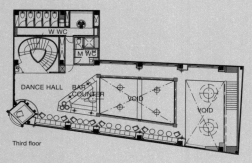

Third floor

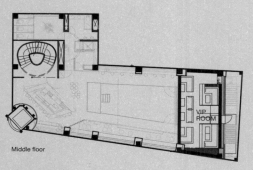

Middle floor

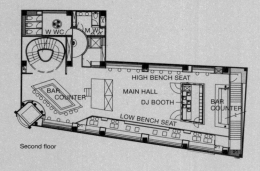

Second floor

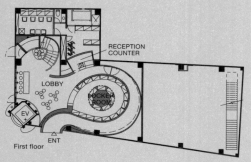

First floor

danceteria SAZA*E: Floor plan

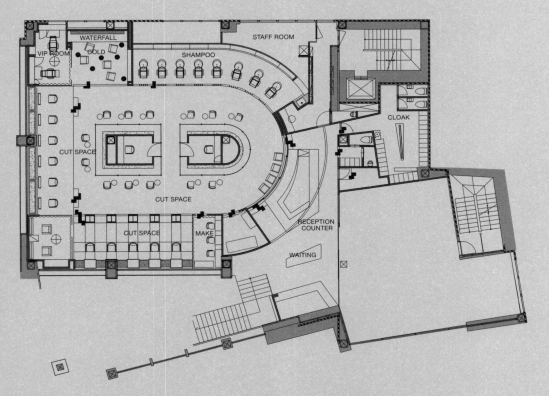

K-two Aoyama: Floor plan

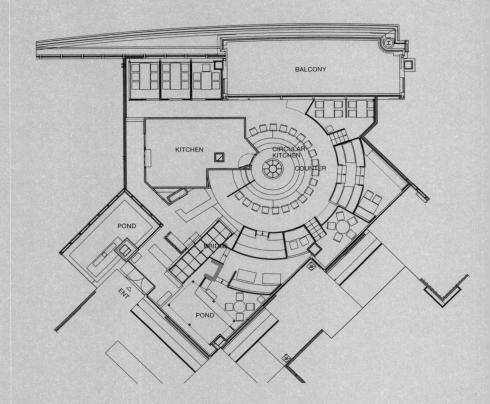

Bishoku MAIMON Umeda: Floor plan

10/
CURIOSITY
Gwenael Nicolas

P100
Mars The Salon

Principal use: Nail salon
Location: Minami-Aoyama,
Minato-ku, Tokyo
Completion date: 2003
Total floor area: 176 square meters,
terrace 52 square meters
Description: A nail salon targeting the
upper echelons of the market, and
offering only private rooms, each one
looking out onto lush gardens beyond
the terrace and featuring the same
teak flooring, making clients feel their
room extends onto the deck. Every
room leaves a different impression via
differences in size and level. All the
furniture features original designs and
the sofas recline to 180 degrees.
Attention has been paid to every detail
to ensure that the space not only looks
stunning, but the service remains
impeccable.

P101
**NISSAN 39th Tokyo Motor Show
Booth**

Principal use: Exhibition booth
Location: Makuhari, Chiba City,
Chiba Prefecture
Completion date: 2005
Total floor area: 3000 square meters
Cooperation:
Management/TBWA/HAKUHODO Inc.,
Direction/Soars International, inc.
Description: Sculptural rings of light
and illuminated paper walls give
physical form to both warmth and the
cool image of technology. Long,
semicircular monitors form an effective
device to connect individual sections
of the interior.

P102
C-1

Principal use: Studio and residence
Location: Shibuya-ku, Tokyo
Completion date: 2005
Site area: 189.51 square meters
Building area: 113.19 square meters
Total floor area: 402.03 square meters
Type of structure: Steel frame, part
reinforced concrete, one floor below
ground, three floors above ground
Structural design: Mitsuhiro Kanada
Facility design: Tact Comfort Co.
Collaborative architectural design:
Tomoyuki Utsumi/Milligram
architectural studio
Cooperation: Kitchen/Kitchenhouse
Description: The designer for this
project reappraised the normal design
process for a house, with its stages of
structure-to-interior-to-furniture,
looking instead at the movements and
changing gaze of the people who live
there, and questioning the relationship
of himself and his family with the
space and with its objects. He choose
to emphasize the gallery (corridor),
creating a delightful space.

P106
C-2

Principal use: Private residence
Location: Kawaguchi-ko, Nishi-tsuru
County, Yamanashi Prefecture
Completion date: 2006
Site area: 469 square meters
Building area: 73.87 square meters
Total floor area: 84.38 square meters
Type of structure: Timber construction,
two floors
Structural design: Niitsugumi
Description: Constructed on a sloping
site, this structure is only a single
story, yet towers over you like a
bridge. Dropping the floor level in the
kitchen encourages conversation by
bringing the person cooking to the
same height as the person reclining on
the sofa. The basement houses a
bedroom and bathroom with sunken
bathtub that looks out onto a scenic
view.

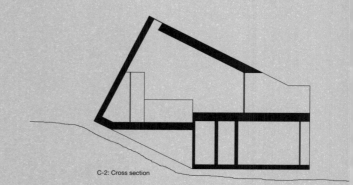

C-2: Cross section

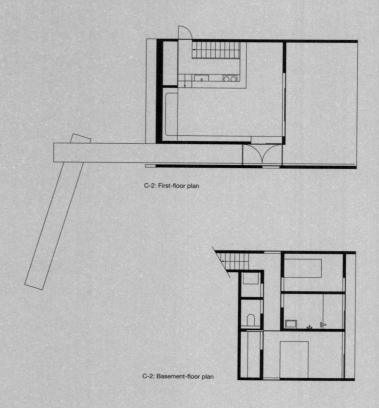

C-2: First-floor plan

C-2: Basement-floor plan

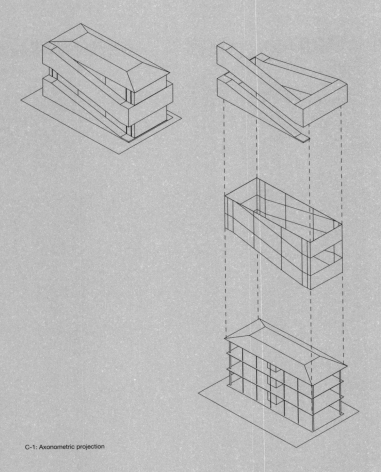

C-1: Axonometric projection

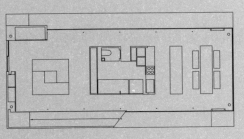

Middle floor

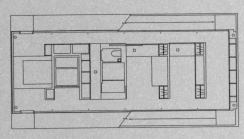

Second floor

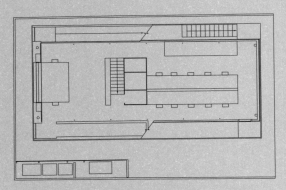

First floor

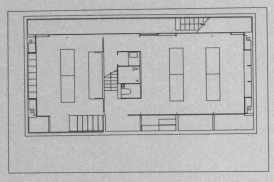

C-1: Basement-floor plan

1/250

11/
Office of
Ryue Nishizawa
Ryue Nishizawa

P110
Funabashi Apartment

Principal use: Apartment block
Location: Higashi-Funabashi,
Funabashi City, Chiba Prefecture
Completion date: 2004
Site area: 339.74 square meters
Building area: 243.04 square meters
Total floor area: 648.90 square meters
Type of structure: Reinforced concrete
construction, three floors above
ground
Structural design: Kume Structural
Research: Development Office
Description: In a block housing 15 rental
apartments measuring 30 square meters
each, the designer proposed splitting
every apartment into three zones,
increasing the sizes of bathrooms and
kitchens to increase their potential. On
one level, the aim was to create a
space that felt like it had three living
rooms.

P112
Moriyama House

Principal use: Private residence and
apartment block
Location: Tokyo
Completion date: 2005
Site area: 290.07 square meters
Building area: 130.09 square meters
Total floor area: 263.32 square meters
Type of structure: Steel construction,
three floors above ground, one floor
below ground
Structural design: Structured
Environment
Description: The owner's house and
four small apartments have been
positioned around the same site to
preserve small gardens between the
diverse buildings. Rather than a
lifestyle closed off from the outside,
this cluster of houses creates a living
environment rich in gardens and
alleyways befitting the metropolis.

P116
**21st Century Museum of
Contemporary Art, Kanazawa**

Principal use: Art museum
Location: Hirosaka, Kanazawa City,
Ishikawa Prefecture
Completion date: 2004
Site area: 26,009.61 square meters
Building area: 9,651.99 square meters
(art museum)
Total floor area: 17,363 square meters
(art museum)
Type of structure: Steel construction
with reinforced concrete, part steel-
framed reinforced concrete, two floors
below ground, two floors above
ground
Structural design: Sasaki Structural
Consultants
Description: Boasting four entrances,
this circular structure has a diameter of
113 meters and contains four courtyards. The central art museum zone
has 19 galleries of varying proportions,
the majority of which feature glass
ceilings. Space has been left between
them and they are not connected,
giving visitors the freedom to visit them
in any order. (Project with SANAA)

P117
Dior Omotesando

Principal use: Boutique
Location: Jingu-Mae,
Shibuya-ku, Tokyo
Completion date: 2003
Site area: 314.51 square meters
Building area: 274.02 square meters
Total floor area: 1,492.01 square
meters
Type of structure: Steel construction
with reinforced concrete, four floors
above ground, one floor below ground
Structural design: Sasaki Structural
Consultants
Description: A boutique in which the
ceiling height varies according to the
floor, reducing the density of the
space. Behind the windows acrylic
screens sculpted like drapes create a
mellow atmosphere. (Project with
SANAA)

P118
Learning Center, EPFL

Principal use: Library, research
facilities, restaurant, exhibition and
event space
Location: Lausanne, Switzerland
Completion date: Completion
expected 2009
Building area: 21,323.25 square
meters
Total floor area: 37,072.90 square
meters
Type of structure: Reinforced concrete
construction, with steel frame, one
floor above ground, one floor below
ground
Design cooperation: SAPS/Sasaki and
Partners, Proplaning AG, B+G
ingenieure Bollinger und Grohmann
GmBH, Walther Mory Maier
Bauingenieure AG, Enerconom
planungs AG, Scherler SA. Ingénieurs-
conseils, SORANE, Enner Pfenninger
Partners AG, Gilbert Monay,
transitecIngeénieure-Conseils SA, Art
Light GmBH
Description: A learning center planned
for the Swiss Federal Institute of
Technology in Lausanne. It consists of
a single-story one-room structure
measuring 175.5 by 121.5 meters. The
space, created for a learning program
with a radically different character,
unfolds in a series of level changes
and courtyards of various sizes.
(Project with SANAA)

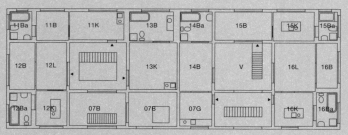

Third floor

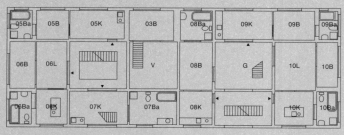

Second floor

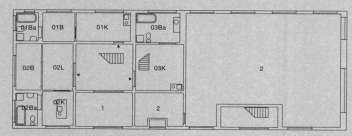

Funabashi Apartment: First-floor plan

K: Kitchen room
L: Living room
B: Bedroom
Ba: Bathroom
G: Garden
V: Void
1:   Entrance
2:   Storage

1/300

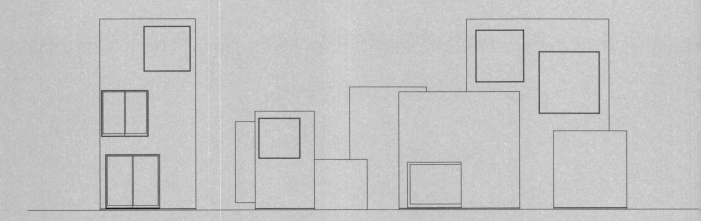

Moriyama House: Elevation

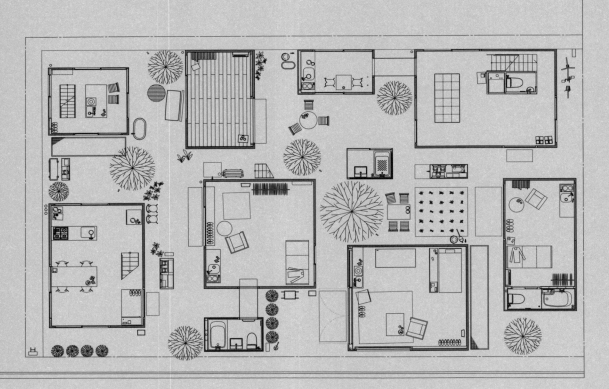

Moriyama House: Floor plan   1/150   N

12/
Wonderwall Inc.
Masamichi Katayama

13/
NAYA architects
Manabu Naya +
Arata Naya

P122
100% ChocolateCafe.

Principal use: Café
Location: Kyobashi, Chuo-ku, Tokyo
Completion date: 2004
Cooperation: Design producer/Koichi
Ando (Ando GALLERY), Art direction
and design/groovisions
Total floor area: 65.4 square meters
Description: This space, a ground-floor
café located in the head offices of a
confectionary manufacturer, is made
to look like a chocolate workshop.
Tables arranged to seem as though
customers have been invited into the
chef's kitchen. A glass display case
entirely covering one wall is filled with
blocks of chocolate: 56 varieties in all.

P124
inhabitant

Principal use: Boutique
Location: Jingu-Mae,
Shibuya-ku, Tokyo
Completion date: 2004
Total floor area: Interior 84.3 square
meters, exterior 17.2 square meters
Description: Themed along the lines of
a Japanese house, the space reveals a
rock garden with a 2-D Mt Fuji
reflected to infinity behind the sliding
doors of the entrance. Downstairs, a
natural scene has been constructed,
transporting you to another dimension.
The bold use of photos of Fuji, a
symbol of Japan, combines with other
classic elements such as tortoiseshell
to create an interior that feels fresh
rather than dated.

P125
THE TOKYO TOWERS,
Sea Sky Guest 49th & 50th Floors

Principal use: Guest rooms for
residents
Location: Kachidoki, Chuo-ku, Tokyo
Completion date: 2005 (Project
completion expected 2008)
Description: Design for the public
space and guestrooms on the 49th and
50th floors of a condo tower block,
featuring a window-side Jacuzzi under
an open atrium space. Completion
planned for 2008.

P126
BAPEXCLUSIVE®

Principal use: Boutique
Location: Minami-Aoyama,
Minato-ku, Tokyo
Completion date: 2005
Total floor area: First and second floors
290.4 square meters, Terrace 31.91
square meters
Description: A lean space unified by a
white grid pattern. Sneakers are set
into the walls of the second floor; the
carpet below is made of squares of 10
different hues. A lighting system and
mirrors direct changing colors of light
onto the connecting staircase. Behind
a glass cylinder, sneakers revolve in a
display made to resemble a baggage
claim conveyor belt; the mirrored
ceiling allows them to be glimpsed on
the floor below through the void space.

P129
Stair

Principal use: Restaurant and lounge
Location: Minami-Aoyama,
Minato-ku, Tokyo
Completion date: 2005
Total floor area: 199 square meters
Cooperation: Custom paint/Masataka
Kurashina (studio DESGOTH)
Description: A sophisticated lounge
whose theme is the glittering days of
cabaret. Constructed out of traditional
materials such as marble and rosewood,
the interior also features tattoo-like
paintings by Masataka Kurashina

P130
HYSTERIC GLAMOUR
Roppongi Hills

Principal use: Boutique
Location: Roppongi, Minato-ku, Tokyo
Completion date: 2006
Total floor area: 413.9 square meters
Description: Glass etches an indistinct
boundary between interior and street
in this boutique, which is divided into
zones to distinguish between the many
labels available, yet still retain visual
harmony throughout. Amongst other
features, rivets in the polished ceiling
help create a look bordering on
excess, accentuating the luxurious feel
of the goods.

P131
OriginalFake

Principal use: Store
Location: Minami-Aoyama,
Minato-ku, Tokyo
Completion date: 2006
Character Object: Gelchop
Total floor area: 128.8 square meters
Description: In this interior, created in
collaboration with New York artist
KAWS, the space consists of two
opposing halves, much like the store
name. An interesting detail is the teeth
shapes on the ceiling.

P136
HOUCHINROU

Principal use: Chinese restaurant
Location: Kawasaki City,
Kanagawa Prefecture
Completion date: 2001
Site area: 99.18 square meters
Building area: 85.97 square meters
Total floor area: 154.37 square meters
Type of structure: Steel construction,
three floors above ground
Structural design: Chi Structural
Design
Description: In order to maximize
interior space, the exterior walls of this
space were made as thin as possible
and erected on the outer limits of the
lot. The structure is held up by N-
shaped units to form a tunnel shape
leading in from the frontage road.
Corten panels were used on the
exterior walls and floor, while the
columns and beams were sandwiched
between calcium silicate boards to
create a simple, flat surface. Out of a
shopping street you could see
anywhere in Japan this façade
appears, floating mysteriously.

P137
House in Futakoshinchi

Principal use: Private residence
Location: Kawasaki City,
Kanagawa Prefecture
Completion date: 2004
Site area: 107.66 square meters
Building area: 52.35 square meters
Total floor area: 88.02 square meters
Type of structure: Cantilevered
reinforced-concrete rigid-frame
construction, two floors above ground
Structural design: Chi Structural
Design
Description: The pole section on this
flagpole-shaped lot, hemmed in by
other houses, extends for 15 meters.
Inside the large structure exist four
levels, with floors freely positioned
rather than being dictated by clearly
defined stories and rooms; spaces are
loosely connected both vertically and
horizontally. Supported by cantilevered
walls, the roof and floors are made of
wood. Storage units are made of steel
plate and set into the concrete
skeleton in the same way as a sash.

P138
House in Edogawa

Principal use: Private residence
Location: Edogawa-ku, Tokyo
Completion date: 2005
Site area: 198.63 square meters
Building area: 80.92 square meters
Total floor area: 284.51 square meters
Type of structure: Steel construction
with steel-reinforced concrete and
reinforced concrete, one floor below
ground, three floors above ground
Structural design: Chi Structural
Design
Description: To the south side of this
lot lies a road and overhead railway, so
ventilation was brought in from the
opposite side, and the entire structure
designed to look like cross-sections of
a railroad car. Above the basement
studio there is a salon, with dry areas
on both sides to bring in light.

P140
House in Tamagawadai

Principal use: Private residence
Location: Setagaya-ku, Tokyo
Completion date: 2005
Site area: 106.09 square meters
Building area: 53.03 square meters
Total floor area: 130.31 square meters
Type of structure: Steel construction,
Part-RC, one floor below ground, two
floors above ground
Structural design: Chi Structural
Design
Description: Rather than slicing a
single block into various rooms, this
house is composed of a series of
rooms stacked up like separate blocks.
Since the size and shape of each block
is dictated by the purpose of the room,
small crevices appear alongside
protrusions and shelves: these have
been transformed into balconies and a
terrace, as well as windows and other
openings that let in light and air, and
afford a view onto the outside world.
Inside, the accumulation of changing
scales and positions of the rooms can
be clearly felt.

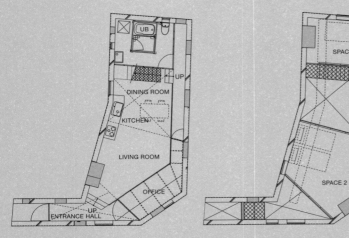

House in Futakoshinchi: First-floor plan

House in Futakoshinchi: Second-floor plan

1/200

N

HOUCHINROU: Cross section

1/200

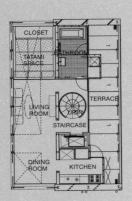

House in Edogawa: Third-floor plan

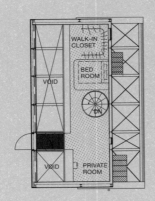

House in Edogawa: Second-floor plan

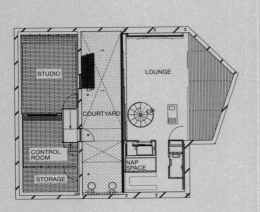

House in Edogawa: Basement-floor plan

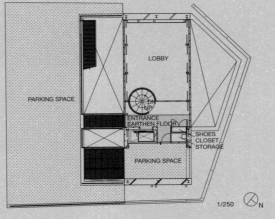

House in Edogawa: First-floor plan

1/250

N

14/
C.C.DESIGN Inc.
Claudio Colucci

P144
VIENS VIENS

Principal use: Nail salon
Location: Daikanyama,
Shibuya-ku, Tokyo
Completion date: 2004
Total floor area: 81.5 square meters
Cooperation: Lighting design/Naiki
Design Office
Description: A nail salon to be frequented by jet setters flying around the globe. Its streamlined curves were based on the image of a plane. The implication is that first class service awaits.

P145
delicabar

Principal use: Patisserie store and café
Location: Paris, France
Completion date: 2003
Total floor area: 140.9 square meters
Cooperation: Lighting design/Nathalie Rozot and Raymond Belle
Confectioner: Sébastien Gaudard
Coordination: Hélène Samuel
Terrace: Space produce/Claudio Colucci Design
Terrace bench: BD LOVE BENCH designed by Ross Lovegrove
Terrace chair: Chair one designed by Constantin Grcic
Description: Located on the second floor of Paris department store Bon Marché, in the La Grande Epicerie de Paris food hall, this café was designed with the keywords "cheeky" and "imagination" in mind. Oversized furniture gives visitors the excited feeling of being children again.

P146
lafuma

Principal use: Boutique
Location: Jingu-Mae,
Shibuya-ku, Tokyo
Completion date: 2005
Total floor area: 189.5 square meters
Cooperation: Artist for artwork on the wall/Isabelle de Scitivaux, Lighting design/Koizumi Lighting Technology Corp.
Description: An exterior box in the brand color of vivid orange, with works of art on display in recognition of the label's cultural side. The entrance is a plain and simple space inserted between the exterior and bold, colorful interior.

P147
Roll Madu

Principal use: Café
Location: Umeda, Kita, Osaka
Completion date: 2004
Total floor area: 202 square meters
Cooperation: Lighting design/Koizumi Lighting Technology Corp.
Description: Inspired by Swiss cake rolls, this interior emulates their shape. The curved walls leading to the cashier's counter are covered in tiny ceramic tiles, with the cakes lined up like precious jewels on one side. A large orange screen made of fabric hangs down in the alcove area, making it feel as though you are gazing at a sunset from underneath a bridge.

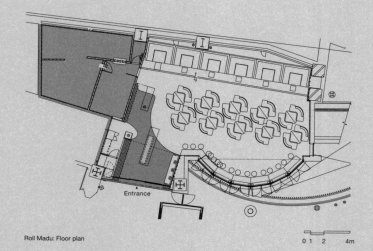

Roll Madu: Floor plan

0 1 2   4m

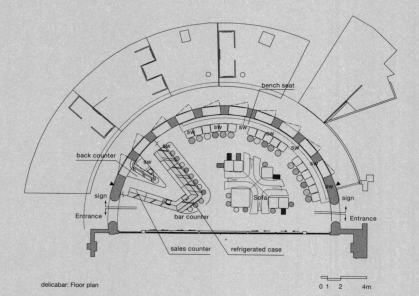

delicabar: Floor plan

0 1 2   4m

15/
Klein Dytham
architecture
Astrid Klein +
Mark Dytham

P151
LEAF Chapel

Principal use: Chapel
Location: Kobuchizawa Town,
Kitakoma County, Yamanashi
Prefecture
Completion date: 2004
Total floor area: 167.887 square
meters
Building area: 121.676 square meters
Type of structure: Steel construction,
Part-RC, one floor above ground
Structural design: Arup JAPAN
Facility design: Tetens Engineering Co.
Cooperation: Lighting design/ICE,
Landscape design/Studio On Site
Description: A wedding chapel taking
up one corner of Risonare, a resort
hotel in Kobuchizawa, Yamanashi.
Reminiscent of a bride's veil, the
image is two leaves curled in on each
other, a delicate lace pattern traced by
roughly 4,700 holes punched in the
white, polycarbonate-capped steel
over the glass roof. At the crowning
point of the ceremony, the steel veil is
lifted to reveal nature all around.
Despite weighing 11 tons, it gives the
impression of being much lighter,
taking around 40 seconds to open
fully.

P154
BRILLARE

Principal use: Party space
Location: Kobuchizawa Town,
Kitakoma County, Yamanashi
Prefecture
Completion date: 2005
Total floor area: 124.44 square meters
Structural design: Arup JAPAN
Facility design: Arup JAPAN
Cooperation: Lighting design/ICE
Description: Risonare's wedding
reception venue. The pre-existing U-
shaped building was remodeled and a
long dining hall extension added to
take it from the courtyard into the
surrounding forest. A cantilevered
structure covered in mirrored
spandrels, it features massive windows
running down both sides. A maximum
of 44 guests can be seated at the 18
meter-long dining table inside.

P157
GAO

Principal use: Activity center
Location: Kobuchizawa Town,
Kitakoma County, Yamanashi
Prefecture
Completion date: 2005
Total floor area: 546 square meters
Description: A children's activity and
day-care center offering art activities,
walks, horse riding and so on to
children at the Risonare resort. To
make it feel like the outdoors, cross-
sections of logs are stacked up the
walls, accented by colorful doors.

P157
BOOKS & CAFE

Principal use: Café and bookstore
Location: Kobuchizawa Town,
Kitakoma County, Yamanashi
Prefecture
Completion date: 2005
Total floor area: 174 square meters
Description: This interior on the
Risonare development is themed on
the Yatsugatake mountain peaks,
forests, and lush greenery; rich wood
grains feature prominently in the
bookshelves and floor, and the store
primarily stocks books about nature.

P157
YY grill

Principal use: Barbecue restaurant
Location: Kobuchizawa Town,
Kitakoma County, Yamanashi
Prefecture
Completion date: 2005
Total floor area: 795 square meters
Cooperation: Lighting design/ICE
Description: A casual restaurant in the
Risonare complex. Taking a forest
motif, wooden silhouettes in the shape
of trees are entwined with mirrors to
produce a feeling of depth. Acorns and
oak leaves have been burnt into the
floor and tables, while the patterned
screen on the ceiling boasts a branch
design.

P158
UNIQLO Ginza

Principal use: Boutique
Location: Ginza, Chuo-ku, Tokyo
Completion date: 2005
Total floor area: 2,543 square meters
Description: A façade designed to
draw the eye in an area full of brand-
name shops. The brightness of each of
the 1000 cells can be controlled
individually, while the steel of the
façade softly reflects the light from
inside to make the logo glitter. Color
schemes were chosen for each area
and the apparel displayed on modular
hanging racks and low tables in an
interior that breaks with tradition.

P159
BILLBOARD Building

Principal use: Accessory shop
Location: Moto-Azabu,
Minato-ku, Tokyo
Completion date: 2005
Site area: 22.51 square meters
Building area: 18.82 square meters
Total floor area: 37.87 square meters
Type of structure: Steel construction,
two floors
Structural design: Structured
Environment
Description: The plan for this lot,
measuring a mere 11 meters wide by
2.5 meters deep, yet in an excellent
position next to an intersection linking
Hiroo, Azabu, and Roppongi, was to
erect a building that would function as
both accessory shop and billboard.
The roof, floor, beams and columns
were made into steel-frame units in the
factory and welded together on site.
Then, the six-meter-tall glass façade
was affixed to the skeleton using
structure sealant. The contrast of light
and color produces interesting effects
in the interior as well, and gives the
building a strong presence.

P160
HEIDI House

Principal use: Residence and office
Location: Shibuya-ku, Tokyo
Completion date: 2005
Site area: 221.83 square meters
Building area: 101.37 square meters
Total floor area: 158.51 square meters
Type of structure: Timber construction,
two floors
Structural design: Structured
Environment
Description: Constructing the exterior
walls out of a timber frame coupled
with structural plywood gave this
structure rigidity. A glass façade was
also added to the outside. Since the
timber frame carries the load, distinctive openings reminiscent of
houses in the Alps could be cut into
the narrow sections between the
supports. Though there are countless
timber-frame houses in Japan, they
can be hard to spot as they are often
clad in fake brickwork and tiles. This
façade wears its witty pattern and
wooden frame with pride.

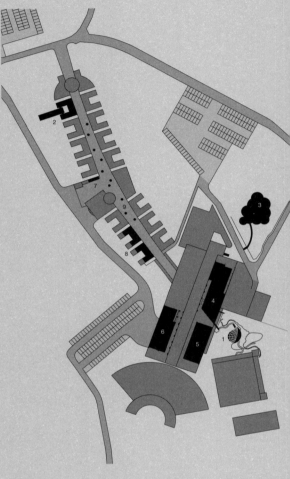

Risonare: Overall view

1. LEAF Chapel
2. BRILLARE
3. Onyoku
4. Y Y grill
5. BOOKS & CAFE
6. GAO
7. Maruyama Coffee
8. Guest Room
9. Machinami Pad

16/
Hitoshi Abe

P164
SBP

Principal use: Bridge
Location: Choshigamori, Shiroishi City,
Miyagi Prefecture
Completion date: 1994
Total floor area: 960.5 square meters
Type of structure: Steel construction
Structural design: Asia Kousoku
Description: The form of this bridge
embodies regulations governing the
site, making invisible rules tangible.
The locus of elements that cleared the
regulations has found form in the
bridge.

P165
KAP

Principal use: Assembly hall
Location: Reihoku Town, Amakusa
County, Kumamoto Prefecture
Completion date: 2002
Site area: 3840.14 square meters
Building area: 934.7 square meters
Total floor area: 993.36 square meters
Type of structure: Timber construction,
Steel construction, two floors above
ground
Structural design: TIS & Partners
Facility design: SOGO
CONSULTANTS, Tohoku
Description: A compact, multi-purpose
hall blending the functions of a town
hall and community center, this design
makes the use of space more efficient,
sparking new activities and bringing
life back to the site.

P166
AIP

Principal use: Restaurant
Location: Kokubun-cho, Aoba-ku,
Sendai City, Miyagi Prefecture
Completion date: 2005
Site area: 208.01 square meters
Building area: 169.16 square meters
Total floor area: 220.37 square meters
Type of structure: Seven floors above
ground
Structural design: Arup JAPAN
Facility design: SOGO
CONSULTANTS, Tohoku
Description: The remodeling of a
French restaurant taking up the first
and second floors of a building. A thin
inner wall of steel panels was inserted
and patterned with zelkova trees, the
symbol of the town, creating a supple
boundary within the space.

P168
SSM

Principal use: Art museum
Location: Tamagawa, Shiogama City,
Miyagi Prefecture
Completion date: 2005
Site area: 638.49 square meters
Building area: 119.94 square meters
Total floor area: 218.89 square meters
Type of structure: Steel construction,
RC construction, one floor below
ground, two floors above ground
Structural design: Structural Design
Office OAK
Facility design: SOGO
CONSULTANTS, Tohoku
Description: 8 sculpture galleries (cells)
were introduced into a pre-determined
volume measuring 10 by 12 by 10
meters, their size and position modeled
on a cluster of soap bubbles. Visitors
experience the sculptures as they walk
around the many-leveled space.

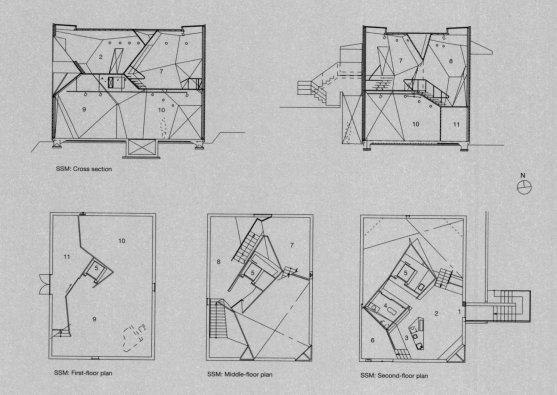

SSM: Cross section

SSM: First-floor plan

SSM: Middle-floor plan

SSM: Second-floor plan

1: Entrance
2: Gallery1
3: Kitchen
4: WC
5: EV
6: Storage-1
7: Gallery2
8: Gallery3
9: Gallery4
10: Gallery5
11: Storage-2

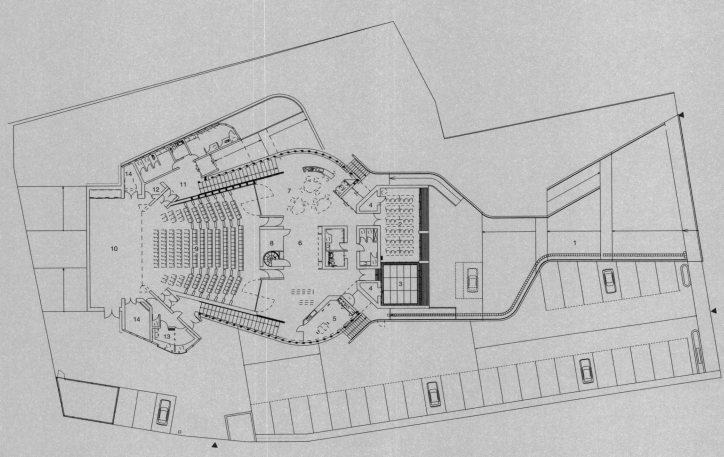

KAP: Ground plan

N

1: Approach
2: Meeting room-1
3: Meeting room-2
4: Closet
5: Office
6: Information space
7: Serving space
8: Volunteer salon
9: Auditorium
10: Stage
11: Foyer
12: Cloakroom
13: Backstage
14: Storage
15: Control room
16: Machine room
17: (A/C) Fan depot

17/
FUMITA DESIGN
OFFICE INC.
Akihito Fumita

P174
NISSAN GALLERY GINZA

Principal use: Car showroom
Location: Ginza, Chuo-ku, Tokyo
Total floor area: 292 square meters
(First floor 197 square meters, Second
floor 95 square meters)
Completion date: 2001
Description: A remodeling project to
establish Nissan's brand identity.
Conceiving cars as "gems," the idea
was to create a fitting showcase to
place them in. The interior features
effective use of steel and aluminum.

P176
m-i-d press

Principal use: Apparel showroom and
Tokyo office
Location: Jingu-Mae,
Shibuya-ku, Tokyo
Total floor area: 359 square meters
(First floor 196 square meters, Second
floor 162 square meters)
Completion date: 2004
Description: A double glass partition
against many of the walls features
around 400 stainless steel lamps
inserted in the interval between the
layers.

P177
H-HOUSE

Principal use: Private residence
Location: Shibuya-ku, Tokyo
Completion date: 2004
Site area: 134 square meters
Building area: 80 square meters
Total floor area: 193 square meters
(Basement floor 75 square meters,
First floor 72 square meters, Second
floor 45 square meters)
Type of structure: Steel construction,
part-reinforced concrete, one floor
below ground, two floors above
ground
Execution design cooperation: MIWA
KANKYO
Description: The interior features many
details usually found in commercial
premises, though functional elements
are hidden as far as possible. A spiral
staircase ascends through the space.

P178
NISSAN GALLERY SAPPORO

Principal use: Car showroom
Location: Chuo-ku, Sapporo City,
Hokkaido
Total floor area: 887 square meters
(First floor 375 square meters, Second
floor 512 square meters)
Completion date: 2004
Description: A car turntable has been
set in the center of the first floor. The
corridors, walls and columns on the
floor above are covered in aluminum
louvers.

P179
ANAYI (Hiroshima Fukuya Ekimae)

Principal use: Boutique
Location: Minami, Hiroshima City,
Hiroshima Prefecture
Total floor area: 66 square meters
Completion date: 2005
Description: Illuminated with indirect
lighting, wooden blocks in warm tones
seem to have gathered in the space
and are being held in stasis. The use of
light as a component is unique.

P180
SPIRITUAL MODE

Principal use: Housing appliance
showroom
Location: Minami-Aoyama,
Minato-ku, Tokyo
Total floor area: 289 square meters
(Basement floor 272 square meters,
First floor 17 square meters)
Completion date: 2005
Description: A showroom for luxury
bath and shower facilities. Fumita also
designed the circular bathtub.

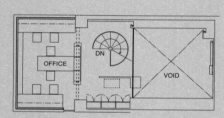

Spiritual Mode: First-floor plan

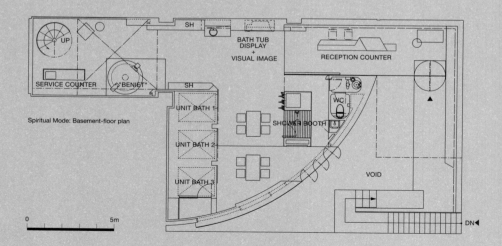

Spiritual Mode: Basement-floor plan

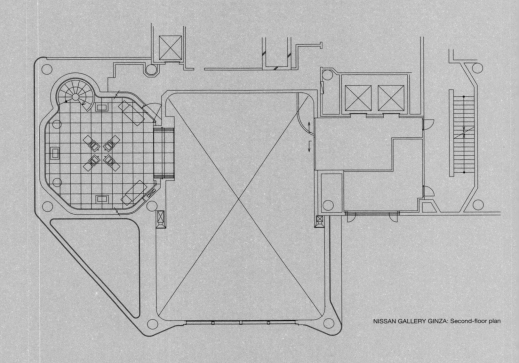

NISSAN GALLERY GINZA: Second-floor plan

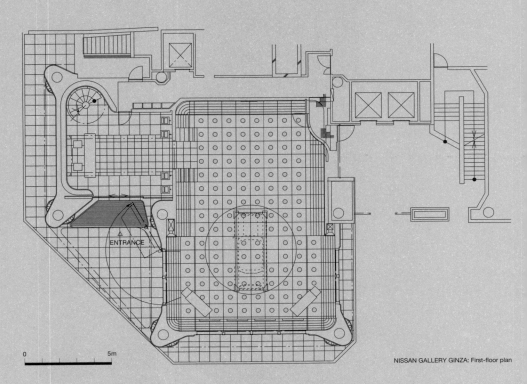

ENTRANCE

0 5m

NISSAN GALLERY GINZA: First-floor plan

18/
Hashimoto Yukio
Design Studio Inc.
Yukio Hashimoto

P186
MINERVA

Principal use: Club
Location: Higashiyama-ku, Kyoto
Completion date: 2004
Total floor area: 247.76 square meters
Type of structure: Timber construction
Cooperation: Lighting/Masanobu
Takeishi (ICE), Custom
lighting/Susumu Ohtsu (B up LTD.)
Description: This pre-existing structure,
a hundred-year-old townhouse, has
been left largely as is, but LEDs and
fiber optics sketch dots onto various
surfaces, although extinguishing them
allows the house's former look to shine
through.

P187
SUIKYOTEI

Principal use: Restaurant and bar
Location: Ginza, Chuo-ku, Tokyo
Completion date: 2005
Total floor area: 486.7 square meters
Cooperation: Lighting/Kimiharu
Nakamae (Noosa design), Custom
lighting/Tohru Katada (STAFF
CORPORATION), Water design/Hitoshi
Yamazaki (HIKARU AQUARIUM CO.,
LTD.), Video images/Kiyoshi Oohori
(Madoka engeering co.,ltd.)
Description: Images of flowing water
are projected onto the floor of the
approach cutting through this space,
creating the illusion you are walking on
water. In one of the private rooms, water
also flows through the table; in another,
there is a pool of water under the glass
floor. Water appears where you least
expect it, creating memorable images
reminiscent of the scene in the
Tarkovsky sci-fi movie Solaris when
the hero's childhood home appears on
the surface of the ocean.

P188
Kamonka UENO

Principal use: Chinese restaurant
Location: Ueno, Taito-ku, Tokyo
Completion date: 2005
Total floor area: 70.82 square meters
Cooperation: Lighting/Masanobu
Takeishi (ICE)
Description: Making it into the structural framework for the interior, this
restaurant emphasizes the approach,
one of the most important elements of
commercial facility design. The
passageway, lit by repeating circles of
tube lighting, runs in a straight line from
the façade: to the left lies the open
kitchen; to the right lies seating
enclosed by latticework screens. At the
far end of the approach, you come to a
labyrinth of different rooms separated
by lattices. One of these features
tables, lighting and furnishings made
entirely out of acrylic, for a clean,
transparent look.

P190
I House

Principal use: Private residence
Location: Inagi City, Tokyo
Completion date: 2005
Total floor area: 137.70 square meters
Cooperation: Lighting/Yoshiyuki
Kobayashi (DAIKO ELECTRIC CO.,
LTD.)
Description: Situated in the countryside
in a place of natural beauty, this house
features a living room, bathroom, and
kitchen facing the outdoors. Picture
windows stand two meters tall under a
three meter-high ceiling, allowing the
owners to admire the scenery.

P191
CHANTO NY

Principal use: Restaurant
Location: New York, USA
Completion date: 2006
Total floor area: 410 square meters
Cooperation: Lighting/Yoshiyuki
Kobayashi (DAIKO ELECTRIC CO.,
LTD.), Custom lighting/Susumu Ohtsu
(B up LTD.)
Description: While preserving a feeling
of the existing building's history, a
selection of Japanese elements in this
restaurant hint at the Orient.
Chandeliers discovered in a local shop,
lacquer walls crafted by Toyama
artisans, and tiny glass lights fitted with
LEDs help fuse Japanese style onto a
New York street.

P192
WATER DROPS

Principal use: Bar
Location: Shinbashi, Minato-ku, Tokyo
Completion date: 2006
Total floor area: 21 square meters
Cooperation: Graphic design/Osamu
Ouchi (nano/nano graphics),
Lighting/Yoshiyuki Kobayashi (DAIKO
ELECTRIC CO., LTD.),
Description: The lips motif produces a
vivid, sensual look. Massive photos of
lips are swathed in tiny water droplets
that seem about to disperse throughout
the bar, thanks to the effect of light
cast on embossed acrylic panels.

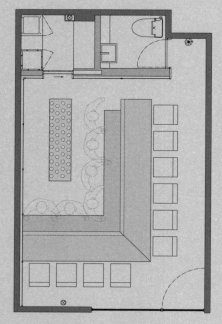

WATER DROPS: Floor plan   1/80

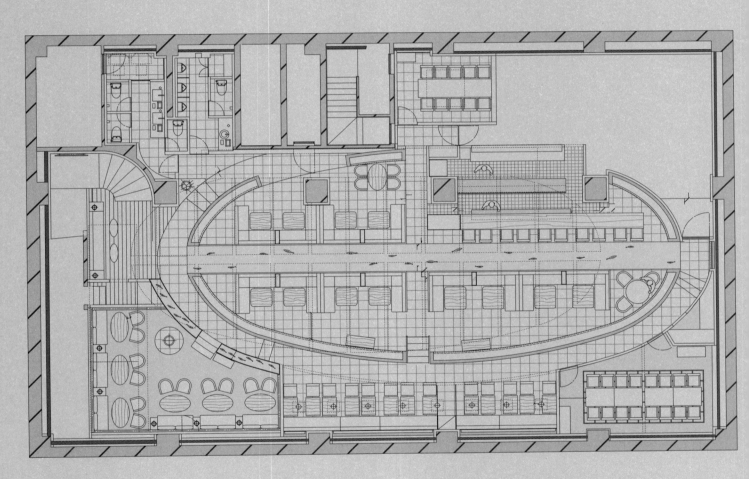

SUIKYOTEI: Floor plan

19/
Noriyuki Otsuka
Design Office Inc.
Noriyuki Otsuka

P195
LE CIEL BLEU Sapporo

Principal use: Boutique
Location: Kita-ku, Sapporo City,
Hokkaido
Completion date: 2005
Total floor area: 125.61 square meters
Cooperation: Book production/
Yoshinori Kikuchi (MOON CROW
STUDIO INC.), Lighting research/
USHIO SPAX INC., Lighting
appliances/LUMINABELLA CO., LTD.,
Sofa/Schiavello Japan Limited, LED
sign/Ohno Research and Development
Laboratories Co., Ltd.
Description: Borrowing the intellectual
look of a library, this interior features a
display of 2,000 snow-white books
with the name of the store embossed
on their spines. The center of the
space has become a relaxing reading
room, complete with custom-made
sofas and carpet, and red pendant
lighting. While the entrance is small, at
2200 millimeters, the bronzed mirrors
on its inner surfaces make it feel more
spacious.

P198
Stunning LURE Shinsaibashi

Principal use: Boutique
Location: Nishi-Shinsaibashi,
Chuo-ku, Osaka
Completion date: 2004
Total floor area: 124 square meters
Cooperation: Tile pattern creation/CPU
corporation, Lighting design/Masaki
Yasuhara /Plus y, Sofa/Schiavello
Japan Limited
Description: Aiming to create a shop
which focuses on the senses of hearing
and touch, the designer for this project
used an ebony shade in the floor and
ceiling and blocked off light from
outside using leather curtains. Ambient
lighting has the low intensity you'd
expect in a restaurant, creating a
relaxed atmosphere that contrasts with
the powerful downlighting in the ceiling
that casts focused spots of light onto
the goods, highlighting their beauty.
The entire space is covered in 10
millimeter mosaic tiles whose pattern
forms an infinity of night-blooming
roses.

P199
axia "X-rated" Omotesando

Principal use: Boutique
Location: Jingu-Mae,
Shibuya-ku, Tokyo
Completion date: 2006
Total floor area: 68.51 square meters
Cooperation: Lighting design/Shinji
Yamaguchi (On & Off inc.), Furniture
production/Schiavello Japan Limited
Description: While stores found inside
malls usually lack the kind of entrance
road-facing stores have, the designer
of Omotesando Hills created a
frontage structure for the basement,
giving the boutiques the added
advantage of an approach. A unique
aspect of this interior is the feeling of
space created by the low-level lighting
reflecting in the mirrored ceiling.

P200
Pleats Box

Principal use: Portable tearoom
Completion date: 2003
Cooperation: Yasuharu Okamoto
(DIMENSION), INOUE PLEATS CO.,
LTD., Masayuki Sakano (SAKANO
DESIGN STUDIO)
Description: A small prefabricated
structure sitting inside another building:
small enough to be transported in a
station wagon, the box takes two
people 30 minutes to erect. Its paper
doors can be slid up and down, their
hatched pattern creating the mood of
the space. Envisaged primarily as a
tearoom, this tiny multi-purpose
structure measures 2500 millimeters
across by 2250 millimeters deep by
2100 millimeters high.

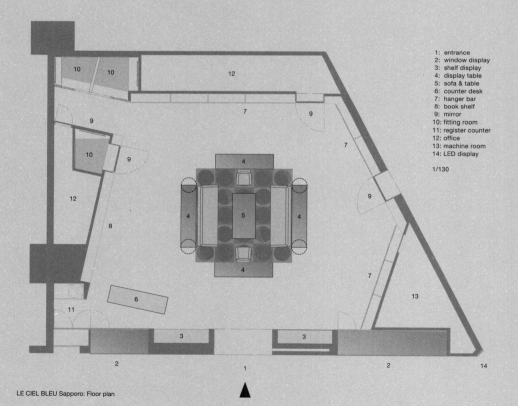

1: entrance
2: window display
3: shelf display
4: display table
5: sofa & table
6: counter desk
7: hanger bar
8: book shelf
9: mirror
10: fitting room
11: register counter
12: office
13: machine room
14: LED display

1/130

LE CIEL BLEU Sapporo: Floor plan

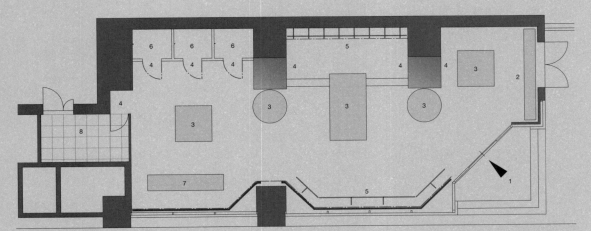

1: entrance
2: sofa
3: display table
4: mirror
5: hanger bar
6: fitting room
7: register counter
8: office

1/150

Stunning LURE Shinsaibashi: Floor plan

1: entrance
2: shelf display
3: hanger bar
4: mirror
5: glass shelf display
6: stool
7: floor lamp
8: accessory counter
9: shoes rack
10: fitting room
11: storeroom
12: stockroom
13: register counter

1/100

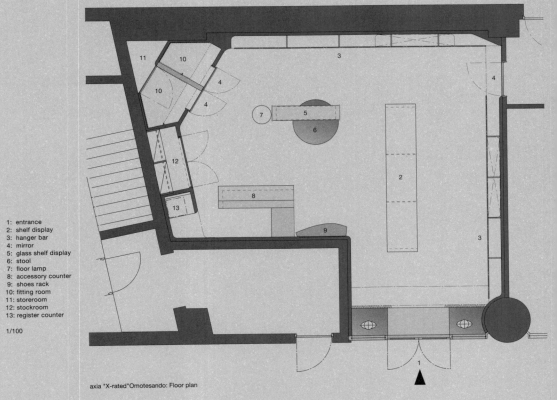

axia "X-rated"Omotesando: Floor plan

20/
Shuhei Endo
Architect Institute
Shuhei Endo

P203
Bubbletecture M

Principal use: Kindergarten
Location: Maibara City,
Shiga Prefecture
Completion date: 2003
Site area: 3,987 square meters
Building area: 1,323 square meters
Total floor area: 1,243 square meters
Type of structure: Timber construction,
RC construction, two floors
Structural design: Mitsuhiro Kanada
(Arup JAPAN)
Description: A kindergarten consisting
of four day-care rooms, a playroom,
staffroom, and conference rooms
whose interlinked dome-shaped
timber-frame roofs extend to delineate
the space required; the largest one
houses the playroom and upstairs
conference rooms. The structure
curves around the playground like a
series of bubbles whose number could
increase to infinity. Rather than glued
laminated timber, the structure is made
from natural wood that can tolerate a
certain amount of distortion.

P205
Bubbletecture O

Principal use: Private residence
Location: Sakai City, Fukui Prefecture
Completion date: 2004
Site area: 140 square meters
Building area: 98 square meters
Total floor area: 227 square meters
Type of structure: Steel construction,
three floors
Structural design: Shinichi Kiyosada
(Kiyosada Structure Office)
Description: Standing in a corner lot
leaving two sides open, this triangular
house is constructed from a series of
trusses to create 19 plane surfaces set
at a variety of angles. The sloping roof,
walls, and windows cause the appearance of both interior and exterior to
change depending on your angle of
view.

P206
Slowtecture Harada

Principal use: Multipurpose assembly
hall
Location: Kamigori Town, Ako County,
Hyogo Prefecture
Completion date: 2004
Site area: 659 square meters
Building area: 65 square meters
Total floor area: 51 square meters
Type of structure: Corrugated steel,
one floor
Structural design: Shinichi Kiyosada
(Kiyosada Structure Office)
Description: Corrugated steel panels
have been curved to create a vaulted,
barrel-shaped interior finished in
wooden planks. The shape softly
articulates its utilitarian function, while
the scenery is brought into the main
room via the large, round entrance.

P207
Rooftecture S

Principal use: Private residence
Location: Tarumi, Kobe City,
Hyogo Prefecture
Completion date: 2005
Site area: 130 square meters
Building area: 50 square meters
Total floor area: 66 square meters
Type of structure: Steel construction,
two floors
Structural design: Masashi Ouji
(Design-Structure Laboratory)
Description: A house for a married
couple that seems to cling to the steep
slope of a lot overlooking Japan's
Inland Sea. The relatively old, stepped
lot is triangular in shape and measures
20 meters from east to west, with its
depth running from 1.5 to 6 meters
due to being sandwiched between
roads snaking up the hill. Behind the
structure, a dry-stone retaining wall
creates a difference in level of 5 to 8
meters between the ground and the
north approach. The house consists of
an artificial surface raised by 5 struts
enveloped by the walls and roof, which
consists of a single oblong bent at an
angle and constructed from folded
metal plate.

P210
BRILLE GINZA RODENSTOCK

Principal use: Optician
Location: Ginza, Chuo-ku, Tokyo
Completion date: 2005
Total floor area: 54 square meters
Description: The stucco wall is composed of a series of flat planes and
curves into which oval shapes have
been cut. The shop displays shelves of
varying sizes, which can be rotated to
reveal mirrors. A composite of cracked
glass and opal film has been used in
the suspended ceiling.

P211
Halftecture OR

Principal use: Restaurant and Public
washrooms
Location: Chuo-ku, Osaka
Completion date: 2006
Site area: 3,091 square meters
Building area: 212 square meters
Total floor area: 228 square meters
Type of structure: Steel construction,
one floor
Structural design: Masashi Ouji
(Design-Structure Laboratory)
Description: This café and washroom
building for use by tourists visiting
Osaka Castle can be found in the
castle grounds. To enable 360-degree
access, the architect went for a
circular shape with central courtyard.
The roof is constructed out of 19-
millimeter anti-corrosion steel welded
into a single panel and supported by
angled columns in sets of three.

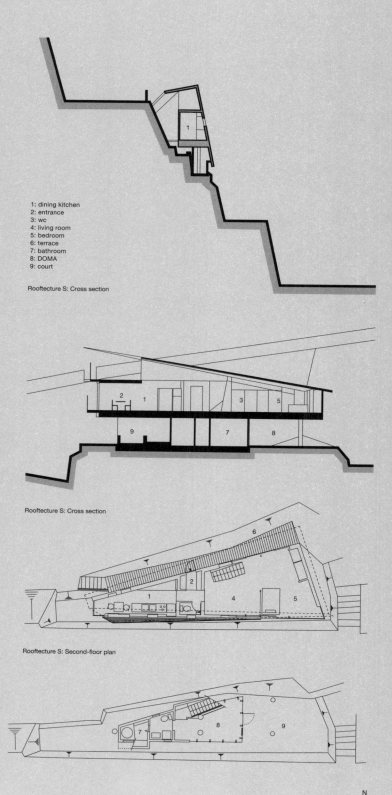

1: dining kitchen
2: entrance
3: wc
4: living room
5: bedroom
6: terrace
7: bathroom
8: DOMA
9: court

Rooftecture S: Cross section

Rooftecture S: Cross section

Rooftecture S: Second-floor plan

Rooftecture S: First-floor plan

0 1 2   5

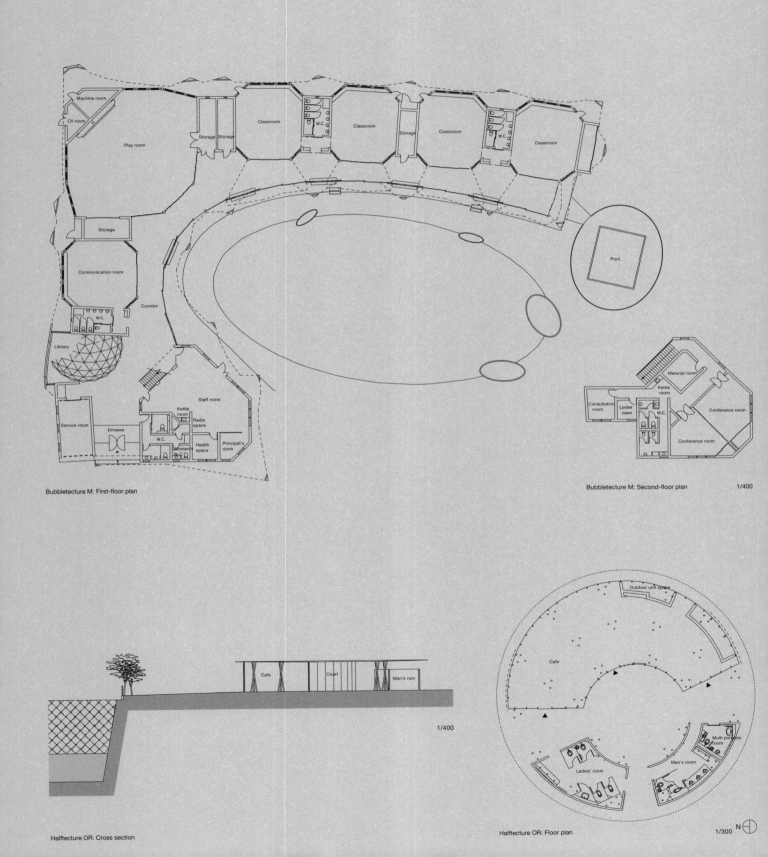

Bubbletecture M: First-floor plan

Bubbletecture M: Second-floor plan   1/400

Halftecture OR: Cross section

1/400

Halftecture OR: Floor plan   1/300   N

21/
Atelier TEKUTO
Yasuhiro Yamashita

P215
Lucky Drops

Principal use: Private residence
Location: Setagaya-ku , Tokyo
Completion date: 2005
Site area: 58.68 square meters
Building area: 21.96 square meters
Total floor area: 60.94 square meters
Type of structure: Steel construction, one floor below ground, two floors above ground
Design: Yasuhiro Yamashita, Shinji Haraguchi, Miki Amano (Atelier Tekuto)
Structural design: Masahiro Ikeda (Masahiro Ikeda Co. Ltd.)
Description: This extremely long, narrow lot stretches for 29.3 meters, with a frontage of 3.26 meters tapering to 0.79 meters at the rear. Added to this, a setback line of 0.5 meters from adjacent lots resulted in a usable width of merely 2 meters. The exterior walls were constructed out of 3 millimeter fiber-reinforced slabs and fireproof sheeting, giving them a transparent quality that allows light to permeate the entire structure. Expanded metal flooring enhances the effect, allowing light and air to filter into the basement.

P218
ref-ring

Principal use: Private residence
Location: Zushi City, Kanagawa Prefecture
Completion date: 2005
Site area: 127.2 square meters
Building area: 54.7 square meters
Total floor area: 64.2 square meters
Type of structure: PCa-PW (pre-stressed wood) construction, two floors
Design: Yasuhiro Yamashita, Junko Hirashita (Atelier Tekuto)
Structural design: Jo ko, Naoyuki Takayama (J. Structual. Design. Co. Ltd.)
Description: This collaborative project with structural designer Joko JSD consists of a prestressed structure composed of 120 by 720 by 3000 by 5000 millimeters panels of laminate timber threaded with pre-stressed concrete steel strands. These panels form two interlocking rings to generate an ecological house that adjusts to different levels of temperature and humidity.

P222
Cell Brick

Principal use: Private residence
Location: Suginami-ku, Tokyo
Completion date: 2004
Site area: 86.60 square meters
Building area: 32.93 square meters
Total floor area: 85.05 square meters
Type of structure: RC construction, Steel construction, one floor below ground, two floors above ground
Design: Yasuhiro Yamashita, Shinji Haraguchi (Atelier TEKUTO)
Structural design: Jun Sato (Jun Sato Structure Engineers)
Description: Thinking how interesting it was that most buildings embody a single solution to the issues of design, functionality, environment, facilities and construction method, the designer found one that was fitting for the tiny lots of land in Japan. Boxes measuring 450 by 900mm in size are used as modules and stacked in a zigzag; they also provide storage space inside. The gaps left at intervals have a depth of 300 millimeters, acting as a brise soleil to reduce glare in the summer, yet also allow winter sunshine to flow in.

P223
Layers

Principal use: Private residence
Location: Setagaya-ku, Tokyo
Completion date: 2005
Site area: 67.14 square meters
Building area: 33.56 square meters
Total floor area: 101.50 square meters
Type of structure: RC construction, timber construction, one floor below ground, two floors above ground.
Design: Yasuhiro Yamashita, Toshinao Iki (Atelier TEKUTO)
Structural design: Jun Sato (Jun Sato Structure Engineers)
Description: A two-story house set on a small, 67-square-meter-plot in a dense residential area. One feature produced by the approach was a series of layers on the exterior walls; these lend depth and density to the space while adding a variety of textures. Timber and plywood were panelized in the factory to reduce transportation and construction costs. The air conditioning system was installed into gaps between the layers to ensure a comfortable living environment. Inside, the aim was to make the house appear more spacious: surfaces also function as layers, freeing them of conventional notions of floor and walls and allowing the space to be grasped as a single entity.

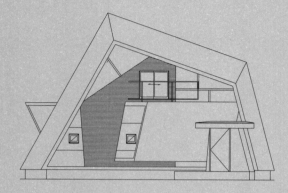

ref-ring: Elevation

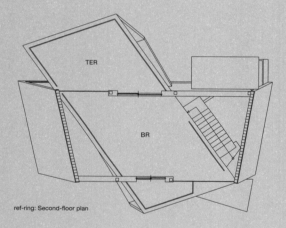

ref-ring: Second-floor plan

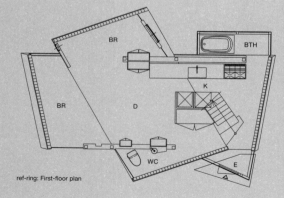

ref-ring: First-floor plan

1/50

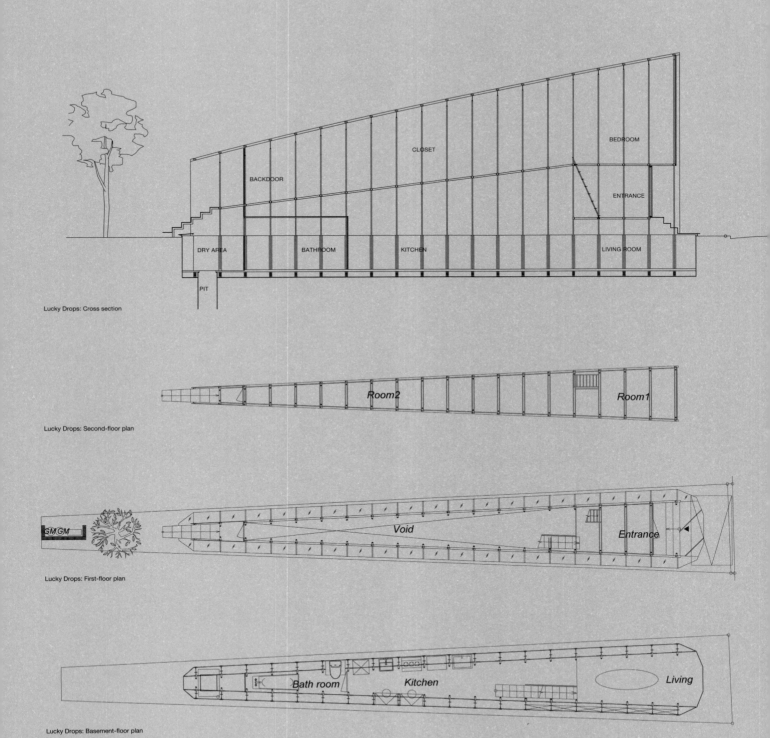

Lucky Drops: Cross section

BACKDOOR

CLOSET

BEDROOM

ENTRANCE

DRY AREA

BATHROOM

KITCHEN

LIVING ROOM

PIT

Lucky Drops: Second-floor plan

Room2

Room1

Lucky Drops: First-floor plan

GMGM

Void

Entrance

Lucky Drops: Basement-floor plan

Bath room

Kitchen

Living

0 500
100 1,000 2,000 3,000 4,000 5,000

N

Biographies

**MOUNT FUJI
ARCHITECTS STUDIO**
Masahiro Harada
Born 1973, Shizuoka Prefecture.
Graduated Shibaura Institute of
Technology Graduate School.
Established MOUNT FUJI
ARCHITECTS STUDIO with MAO
in 2004.
MAO (Mao Harada)
Born 1976, Kanagawa
Prefecture. Graduated Shibaura
Institute of Technology.
Established MOUNT FUJI
ARCHITECTS STUDIO with
Masahiro Harada in 2004.

TORAFU ARCHITECTS
Koichi Suzuno
Born 1973, Kanagawa
Prefecture. Graduated Tokyo
University of Science, Yokohama
National University Graduate
School. Established TORAFU
ARCHITECTS with Shinya
Kamuro in 2004.
Shinya Kamuro
Born 1974, Shimane Prefecture.
Graduated Meiji University
Graduate School MA program.
Established TORAFU
ARCHITECTS with Koichi Suzuno
in 2004.

Hiroshi Nakamura
Born 1974, Tokyo. Graduated
Meiji University Graduate School.
Established NAP Architects in
2002.

TONERICO: INC.
Hiroshi Yoneya
Born 1968, Osaka Prefecture.
Graduated Musashino Art
University. Established
TONERICO: INC. with Ken
Kimizuka and Yumi Masuko in
2002.
Ken Kimizuka
Born 1973, Osaka Prefecture.
Graduated Musashino Art
University Department of
Architecture.
Yumi Masuko
Born 1967, Tokyo. Graduated
Joshibi University of Art and
Design.

Keiichiro Sako
Born 1970 Fukuoka Prefecture.
Graduated Tokyo Institute of
Technology, Yokohama National
University Graduate School.
Established SKSK architects in
2004, joint chairman of Toho
Sekkei Public Corporation.

Takaharu Tezuka
Born 1964, Tokyo. Graduated
Musashi Institute of Technology,
University of Pennsylvania
Graduate School. Co-established
TEZUKA ARCHITECTS with Yui
Tezuka in 1994
Yui Tezuka
Born 1969 Kanagawa Prefecture.
Graduated Musashi Institute of
Technology, exchange student at
University College London
Bartlett School of Architecture.

Yasumichi Morita
Born 1967, Osaka. Established
Morita Yasumichi Design Office
in 1996. Established
GLAMOROUS Co., Ltd. in 2000.

Katsunori Suzuki
Born 1967, Osaka. Graduated
Kyoto Seika University.
Established FANTASTIC DESIGN
WORKS in 2001.

Yoshiyuki Morii
Born 1967, Tokyo. Established
cafe co. in 1996.

Gwenael Nicolas
Born 1966, Brittany, France.
Graduated Ecole Superieure
d'Arts Graphiques et
d'Architecture d'Interieure
(ESAG), Paris, 1988, Royal
College of Art, London.
Established CURIOSITY with
Reiko Miyamoto in 1998.

Ryue Nishizawa
Born 1966, Kanagawa
Prefecture. Graduated Yokohama
National University Graduate
School. Established Sejima And
Nishizawa And Associates
(SANAA) with Kazuyo Sejima in
1995. Established Office of Ryue
Nishizawa in 1997.

Masamichi Katayama
Born 1966, Okayama Prefecture.
Established H. Design
Associates, dissolved H. Design
Associates in 1999. Established
Wonderwall Inc. in 2000.

Manabu Naya
Born 1961, Akita Prefecture.
Graduated Shibaura Institute of
Technology. Established NAYA
architects with Arata Naya in
1993.
Arata Naya
Born 1966, Akita Prefecture.
Graduated Shibaura Institute of
Technology. Established NAYA
architects with Manabu Naya in
1993.

Claudio Colucci
Born 1965, Locarno, Switzerland.
Graduated in Arts Decoratifs,
Geneva, Ecole National
Supérieure de Création
Industrielle, Paris. Exchange
student at Kinston Polytechnic,
UK. Co-founded RADI
DESIGNERS in Paris with three
other designers in 1994.
Established C.C.DESIGN Inc. in
Tokyo and Paris in 2000.

Klein Dytham architecture
Astrid Klein
Born 1962, Varese, Italy.
Graduated Ecole Municipale
Superieure des Arts Decoratifs
de Strasbourg. Graduated Royal
College of Art, London.
Established Klein Dytham
architecture with Mark Dytham in
1991.
Mark Dytham
Born 1964, Northamptonshire,
UK. Graduated Newcastle
University, Royal College of Art,
London. Established Klein
Dytham architecture with Astrid
Klein in 1991.

Hitoshi Abe
Born 1962, Miyagi Prefecture.
Completed M-ARK3 course at
Southern California Institute of
Architecture (SCI-Arc). After
working for Coop Himmelblau's
Los Angeles design office,
established Atelier Hitoshi Abe in
1992. Appointed University of
California, Los Angeles (UCLA)
Professor and Chair, April 2007.

Akihito Fumita
Born 1962, Osaka. Graduated
Osaka University of Arts.
Established FUMITA DESIGN
OFFICE INC. in 1995.

Yukio Hashimoto
Born 1962, Aichi Prefecture.
Graduated Aichi Prefectural
University of Fine Arts and Music.
Established Hashimoto Yukio
Design Studio Co., Ltd. in1996.

Noriyuki Otsuka
Born 1960, Fukui Prefecture.
Graduated design school, 1981.
Traveled in Europe 1981~1982.
Established Noriyuki Otsuka
Design Office Inc. in 1990.

Shuhei Endo
Born 1960, Shiga Prefecture.
Graduated Kyoto City University
of Arts Graduate School.
Established ENDO SHUHEI
Architect Institute in 1988.

Yasuhiro Yamashita
Born 1960, Kagoshima
Prefecture. Graduated Shibaura
Institute of Technology Graduate
School. Established Yamashita
Kai Architectural Design Office in
1991, renamed Atelier TEKUTO in
1995. Established NCS Ltd. in
2004.

Photo Credits

Daichi Ano
18, 24, 27, 28, 29, 99, 100,
102-103, 104, 105, 154-155,
156, 157, 159, 163, 165, 166.
167, 168, 169

Yoshihisa Araki
87, 88

Satoshi Asakawa
36, 37, 38, 39

Shunichi Atami
164

Ryota Atarashi
160

CLAUDIO COLUCCI DESIGN
145

Jimmy Cohrssen
17

CURIOSITY
106

Gregory Goode
132 (Left)

Shigeru Hiraga
140

Hiroyuki Hirai
199, 200

HIROSHI NAKAMURA &
NAP ARCHITECTS CO., LTD.
31 (Lower right), 33

Hitoshi Abe Atelier
171

Jin Hosoya
110 (Above)

Minoru Iwasaki
45, 47, 48, 49, 50, 53

Koichi Kawamura
42

Katsuhisa Kida
56, 57, 58, 59, 60, 61,
62-63, 151, 152, 153

Mori Kohda
136

Francesca Mantovani
145 (Upper right, Lower left,
Lower right)

Yoshiharu Matsumura
203, 204, 205, 206,
207, 208, 209, 211

Akiyoshi Miyashita
New Photo Studio
101

MOUNT FUJI
ARCHITECTS STUDIO
9, 10, 11, 14

Nacása & Partners Inc.
40, 41, 68, 69, 70, 71, 72, 73,
74, 75, 76, 79, 80, 81, 82, 83,
84, 144, 146, 147, 183, 158,
173, 174, 175, 176, 177, 178,
179, 180-181, 182, 186, 187,
188, 189, 190, 191, 192, 210

Nobuaki Nakagawa
23, 30, 31 (Above, Lower left)

Office of
Ryue Nishizawa
114, 115

Tomio Ohashi
46

Yuki Ohmori
20 (Above, Below)

Shigeru Ohno
51

SANAA
(Sejima And Nishizawa And
Associates)
116, 117, 118

Yasunori Shimomura
89, 90, 91, 92, 93, 94, 95

Shinkenchiku-sha
12-13, 19, 109, 110 (Below),
111, 112-113

Mikio Shuto
15, 25, 32, 43, 65, 85, 107,
141, 149, 161, 193, 201, 224

Kozo Takayama
121, 122, 123, 124, 125,
126, 127, 128, 129, 130,
131, 132, 133, 138, 139,
195, 196, 197, 198

Yuji Takeuchi
96

Koui Yaginuma
135, 137

Masayoshi Yamada
76

Makoto Yoshida
215, 216, 217, 218, 219,
220-211, 222, 223

About the author:

Masaaki Takahashi is an independent writer and editor specializing in design, architecture, art, and culture. He is a regular contributor to *AD:Architectural Design*, *Interior Design*, *FRAME* and *MARK* magazines. His work also appears in other international publications such as Interior Design, *Blueprint*, *Design Report*, *IdN*, *MONITOR*, *CUBES* and *Shotenkenchiku*.

Born in Tokyo, Takahashi worked for a variety of companies after graduating from a university in Tokyo, including an electronics industry newspaper and a firm involved in natural language processing. In 1987 he took off for Europe, studying oil painting in Berlin before enrolling in a course in environmental design at the Polytechnic of North London (now London Metropolitan University). A desire to further his studies took him to the Fashion Institute of Technology at The State University of New York, where he graduated in interior design at the same time as taking New York University's international relations course. Returning to Japan, he worked for a time in the editorial department of Shotenkenchiku, a monthly magazine for interior and store design, before establishing his own editorial production company, Brizhead, in 1996.

Authored:
Design City Tokyo (Wiley Academy)

Co-authored books include:
Dress Code (Birkhauser)
Bon Appetit (Birkhauser)
City & Food (Wiley Academy)
Food & Architecture (Wiley Academy)
Club Culture (Wiley Academy)
Progressive Architecture & Urban Development (Wiley Academy)
Tokyo Architecture & Design, and guide series (teNeues)
Tokyo Architecture & Design (Daab)

Translations include:
SHIGERU BAN (PHAIDON Japan)
ARCHITECTURE NOW! Taschen Icons Series (TASCHEN Japan)
ART NOW! Taschen Icons Series (TASCHEN Japan)
Kester Rattenbury, Robert Bevan & Kieran Long, Architects Today (Maruzen)